Bruce Catton, Pulitzer Prize winning author, was America's most popular Civil War historian. He began his career as a journalist, but it was his understanding that wars were made up of the clash of human dreams and passions that made *his* Civil War come alive for millions. Mr. Catton died in 1978.

"Mr. Catton raises history to its most civilized height—where bonds of human sympathy and continuity link the present with the past."

—*HOUSTON CHRONICLE*

BRUCE CATTON

REFLECTIONS ON THE CIVIL WAR

EDITED BY JOHN LEEKLEY

BERKLEY BOOKS, NEW YORK

Photographs of the drawings by Jim Kalett

This Berkley book contains the complete
text of the original hardcover edition.
It has been completely reset in a typeface
designed for easy reading and was printed
from new film.

REFLECTIONS ON THE CIVIL WAR

A Berkley Book / published by arrangement with
Doubleday & Company, Inc.

PRINTING HISTORY
Doubleday edition published 1981
Berkley edition / November 1982

ISBN: 0-425-10495-8

A BERKLEY BOOK ® TM 757,375
Berkley Books are published by The Berkley Publishing Group,
200 Madison Avenue, New York, New York 10016.
The name "Berkley" and the "B" logo
are trademarks belonging to Berkley Publishing Corporation.

PRINTED IN THE UNITED STATES OF AMERICA

10   9

*Grateful acknowledgment is made
to Lou Reda and Lou Reda Productions, Inc.
for their efforts in connection
with the publication of this book.*

Contents

Editor's Foreword

Reflections is a summation of the Civil War themes with which Bruce Catton was most concerned. On every page and between every line one can sense the intimate way in which Bruce understood the experience of that war. He could feel what those soldiers felt because he shared with them the same faith; faith in ourselves as Americans, in what we have done and can do, as a people, as a nation. When we read his work we learn more than the ideas; we gain the experience. In *Reflections* he shares his vision of what the war was all about, and at the same time, reaffirms that faith. We feel his work as much as read it. It is as close as we could come to having a conversation with Bruce Catton.

In this work, Bruce reflects on a wide range of subjects, including the cause and meaning of the Civil War; the actual experience of army life for the common soldier; and the major campaigns. This is not a detailed, formal military history, something that Bruce has already done so well. Here are the broader strokes, the motives and emotions, "the moving currents in the spirits of men" that caused the flood of civil war. In *Reflections* there flow the currents that run deeply through our national consciousness.

Much of this text is based on tape recordings Bruce made some time ago for educational distribution. I had joined him in the process of editing the transcripts of these tapes shortly before his death, at which time I assumed the role of editor. Some reworking and restructuring of the material was necessary to bring what had originated as oral history into a more orderly written presentation, but every effort has been made to preserve the sense of intimacy and warmth of tone.

I came to know Bruce Catton because of a sketchbook, battered and browned with age, drawn by a young private in the Union army, a soldier-artist named John Geyser. Geyser volunteered a few days after Fort Sumter surrendered and served throughout most of the war. He carried this sketchbook through the dark early years of defeat for the North, and in it he drew the people, the land, and the violence around him in a moving and poetic way.

John Geyser was much like other American country boys in 1861, caught up in the Civil War, moved by his ideals to enlist, and carried in a flood he only vaguely understood; a rising river of change that has come down to us today. But John Geyser did realize, along with the men he fought with, and against, that they were involved in a very great event, an Armageddon, and that they were making history; and John Geyser recorded it. With this sensitive record of a life being lived, he has shown us the very human side of history that is often missing from the dry facts of history books.

The sketchbook has survived since 1861, passing through many hands, touching many lives, and was finally acquired and preserved by my father, Richard Leekley, a rare-book dealer specializing in Americana. When he passed away in 1976, the sketchbook came into my hands.

With the slim book of drawings under my arm, I met with Bruce at his favorite haunt, the Algonquin Hotel. I showed him the drawings and we talked about the view of the war through the eyes and heart and hands of this common soldier, John Geyser. Out of that meeting came a shared vision. For almost two years, we met and we "relived" the drawings, with Bruce identifying and elaborating on the actual places of battle and details of army life depicted in the drawings that Geyser had made as an eyewitness. Bruce used these descriptions, together with Geyser's war records, company history, and personal documents, to construct the narrative of John Geyser's journey which appears here as Part Five, *There Was a Young Soldier*.

Bruce was as much a poet as he was a historian, his great narrative power soaring and lyrical. He brought the Civil War to life in a way no other historian has been able to do. His writing and character reflected the same qualities, both straightforward and informal, with great dignity and a faith in other men. Like the Civil War veterans he remembered from his boyhood in Michigan, he embodied the ideals that have sustained America, not only in his virtue and integrity, but in the great judgment he displayed. He was never hesitant to say that while the Civil War was over, the change that it started was not over; the work not finished. He said that we must all live up to what those who came before us have given us, like the veterans of the Civil War. This sense of responsibility as an American is one of the great qualities of Bruce's life and work. With the death of Bruce Catton in the late summer of 1978, we lost a national treasure.

It was a privilege and a pleasure to have known the friendship of Bruce Catton and to have worked with him. His vision has illuminated the path leading to that "dark and indefinite shore," that great unknown national destiny envisioned by Abraham Lincoln in his dreams. The words of Bruce Catton flood that shore with light. He lies now, under the lilacs, with the other

Civil War veterans, in the country cemetery near where
he was born. But his life's work continues to be an inspiration for us, and for the generations to come.

John Leekley

Preface

I have spent a good many years studying the Civil War and trying to find out all that I could learn about it. I suppose, in a way, I am following a trail that I first stumbled onto when I was a small boy back in a little town in Michigan. The old men of that town were Civil War veterans. We used to see a lot of them. On Decoration Day, for instance, there would always be services in the Town Hall, songs, and speeches. The old gentlemen would be sitting there with their blue uniforms and their white beards, and after the services, all hands would go out on the village cemetery to put lilacs on the graves of the veterans who had already passed on.

The old men, simply because they were veterans of the Civil War, gave a color and a tone, not merely to our village life, but to the concept of life with which we grew up. They seemed to speak for a certainty, for an assured viewpoint, for a standard of values that did not fluctuate, that put such things as bravery, patriotism, confidence in the progress of the human race, and the belief

in a broadening freedom for all men, at the very basis of
what men moved by. That faith, in those days seventy
years ago, was a very real, strong thing. It shaped our
lives. I think it was a good thing for the country to have
had such a faith; it has grown a little thin in more recent
years. We have become, perhaps, too wise for our own
good—or if not too wise, too sophisticated. We find it
harder to believe in the things the Civil War veterans
stood for, in the things the war itself won for the entire
country. And I think we've lost something that we need
very much to regain. In following up the story of the
war, I think I was always subconsciously driven by an
attempt to restate that faith and to show where it was
properly grounded, how it grew out of what a great
many young men on both sides felt and believed and
were brave enough to do on the basis of their feelings
and their beliefs.

Perhaps by examining the war closely, by realizing
both what it cost and what it won for mankind as a
whole, we can get back a little of that earlier faith, that
confidence that, as Americans, we are somehow on the
right path, and that while our final goal is still clouded
and hidden from view, we can at least feel sure that it
will be worth reaching.

To tell the story of the war, by itself, is not enough. It
is necessary to understand what it grew out of—what
emotions, antagonisms, and moving currents in the
spirits of men brought it forth; how the different
viewpoints, North and South, became irreconcilable so
that the men of the two sections felt moved to go out
and fight and die in defense of their own beliefs. It is not
sufficient to speak only of the military campaigns, but
also of things that happened behind the lines; the
currents that flowed through men's emotions; the
development of industry, of economics, of agriculture,
of science and invention that went on during the war
and had their effect on it.

In the end, of course, the country that came out of the
war was very different from the one that went into
it—not merely because the war had been fought and had

caused much damage and destruction, but because America itself had been developing all during the time it was fighting. In these pages we will explore some of those aspects of development, how they moved and what they did to us, so that we can perhaps see how the America of, say, 1870, differed from the America of 1850. It was not just the war that made the change. It was a moving tide that was flowing down the century and which is still operating in America—a tide of development, expansion, and rising expectations.

Bruce Catton

Introduction

"What we shall some day become will grow inexorably out of what today we are; and what we are now, in its turn, comes out of what earlier Americans were—out of what they did and thought and dreamed and hoped for, out of their trials and their aspirations, out of their shining victories and their dark and tragic defeats."[*]

With these words Bruce Catton eloquently answered the question "why history?" His belief in the study of history is a philosophy of life we all can heed, for it was the meaning of the past, present, and future that he sought.

We in history are often asked how we became involved, what was our inspiration. I have heard Bruce Catton reply, as he does in these pages, that his interest in the Civil War came from seeing and talking with the aging veterans of the Blue in his boyhood Michigan

---

[*] From an address on the "Lost Colony," Roanoke Island Historical Commission, June 28, 1958, manuscript in Bruce Catton Collection, American Heritage Center, University of Wyoming.

home. But even in this reply one can sense that there was a good deal more to it than that, important though that experience was.

These scenes and voices of his youth, perhaps, triggered an exploring mind that was innately seeking our inheritance, looking for a meaning, or even a lack of meaning, in mankind's saga on this planet.

Catton was always questioning, pondering, inquiring, often hesitant, seldom if ever certain. Never dogmatic, he was at home with the perplexities, the perilousness of life and events. This is clearly shown in these conversations. And they are not a monologue, but seem to have been spoken in a reverie, as if they were not just the thoughts of Catton, but echoes from those thousands that he wrote and talked about, that he lived with in victory and defeat, in suffering and joy.

Catton was the man who not only vitalized a monumental segment of our past, who proved that all varieties of readers can enjoy history, but who was a wondrously endowed teacher, if not often in the formal classroom. His awareness of all of life, his grasp of the all but incomprehensible kaleidoscope of events great and small, of personalities at all levels of endeavor is awesome. In his works he encompasses so much and is so aware of his responsibility to history that he eschews pontification, instead expressing his ideas with profound and inquisitive simplicity.

In these pages we feast on the mature thoughts of Bruce Catton, and this can be a disarming experience. To me, it is as if we are once more on a train, Bruce and I, as we so often were, heading into the darkness of a midwestern night. There in the club car we sit, I the listener. We are aware of the noisy clanking, the jerk and motion of the train, with distant sounds occasionally jarring with muffled suddenness. But Bruce and I are not alone. For somewhere out there in the night are the dusty marching, shuffling feet of Blue and Gray, there are the field commanders deep in worried thought, and there are those in the seats of power in governments North and South, uncertain often, feeling the weight of unrelenting care. There are those left at home, men, women, and children, who are wondering, who live with anxiety. What is happening to their loved ones on the fields of strife, to the sons and husbands so far from home?

This is what I hear when I read these pages. Catton spoke as he wrote; to read him is to hear him. It is clear that in his absorption with the Civil War he did not forget other yesterdays, or today, or the enigma of tomorrow. This is evident on every page of these aptly titled "reflections."

In the many years of our friendship and association, I felt that Catton was always working, always learning. Oh, he enjoyed life. He enjoyed it especially because to him it was so full of history. He was an extremely well disciplined man, he liked what he did, he liked to talk and think history and to listen as well.

He dared to dream and he saw the necessity and value of what has been termed the "grand scene." It seems to me that with the departure of some of the superstars, we are lacking now the historical writers who can tell us about the "grand scene." While not all of them were working exclusively in the "middle-period," or Civil War era, we do not seem to have those with the breadth of vision of James Ford Rhodes, James G. Randall, Douglas Southall Freeman, Allan Nevins, Bruce Catton, and a host of others now gone.

We can be proud of the tellers of our story and we can be proud of the legacy of Bruce Catton. Today Catton is universally recognized as a master of the written word. He was the deft and moving teller and "crier" of the "true story," or at least as close as anyone can get to the truth. I and those who analyze his work seriously can testify to his absolute dedication to the canons of history, to those mysterious "rules of evidence," to the trade and practice of the careful writer and historian. But beyond that is the eternal question mark that any honest man must always face. For Bruce is not only the superb narrator, but the meticulous evaluator turned philosopher.

These attributes have made his contribution to that
deadly-sounding topic historiography immense. With a
benign ignoring of the pedagogue's terms and methods,
Bruce Catton, perhaps unwittingly, through his spoken
and written words created his own historiography and
added glowingly to our treasured record.

I recall on one occasion, upon the publication of his
first major Civil War volume, *Mr. Lincoln's Army*, first
of the trilogy on the Union Army of the Potomac, Catton was asked by one of the literati why he had waited
until he was over fifty to publish his first Civil War
book. His quiet, friendly reply mitigated the presump-
tuousness of the question: "It was written when I was
ready; when I knew I could write it as I saw it."

When he was *ready*. When the tools and the inspiration combined in this affable, warm, genial, easily
approachable man of letters. Yet there was at the same
time about Catton something private, something not
easily reachable. I knew him closely for over a quarter
of a century, worked directly with him on the *Centennial History of the Civil War* for eleven years, and
yet I could never quite get inside the private man. The
reason for this seems clear to me. He needed that
privacy for contemplation, for understanding.

Certainly my wife and I dredged up for him over nine
million words of research notes for the *Centennial
History*. We combed the nation for the fullest possible
picture of the facts and viewpoints of the Civil War. But
it was Catton who did the true research, Catton who did
the thinking and the writing. I stood in awe at his
editorial discrimination, at his extraordinary ability to
digest unwieldy masses of material, and then at the
product that came forth in all the major books, and now
in these thoughts.

His never-ending curiosity shows through all his
works, as it does in *Reflections*. He enunciates in this
work not only the transcendent truths and poses the
perennial unanswerable questions of the Civil War, but
he delves into such deceivingly disparate subjects as the
wounded veterans, the veterans reserve corps, enlist-

ments, the work of the engineers, the art of Private Geyser, the marches, the battles, the esprit de corps, the role of the decision makers. And it all goes to make a unified whole. As the editor wisely points out, what emerges is not a chronologically comprehensive history of the war, but rather an insightful and perceptive excursion into the whole period, its lessons and meaning. Here is a distillation of Catton's years of contemplation on the Civil War.

There is a wonderment to it all, as there was to that period, the "human miracle" as Catton calls it. It may have been on that nonmythical train or at one of his New York haunts that I asked him how he knew about some detail or other of the war. The bright eyes looked out in wonderment, the scraggly moustache twitched, the pencil was chewed a bit more, the martini thoughtfully stirred with a plastic sword, and he replied, not to me, but to all: "I don't know, maybe I was there." Maybe he was.

Catton was a man of many eras and this brought to his thoughts a balance of narrative, feeling, and analysis, coupled with a realistic optimism. To him, as he expresses in *Visions* in this volume, the American man in the long run "is a pretty good man," and "When he sets himself to do something, he will stick with it as long as he can stand on his feet and breathe." At the same time, Catton believed that the cataclysm of the Civil War was worthwhile. "We have not yet reached the goal which we set ourselves at that time and I'm not sure we ever will be satisfied with our progress." There is always a further dream to him. He is forever urging us on.

Bruce Catton was not afraid of being subjective, yet he never deserted the higher aims and responsibilities of history. He could write, as he did in *America Goes to War*, "Forget the swords and roses aspect, the deep sentimental implications, the gloss of romance; here was something to be studied, to be prayed over, and at last to be lived up to."†

† Bruce Catton, *America Goes to War* (Middletown, Conn.: Wesleyan University Press, 1958), p. 12.

That is it, and here we find him once more thinking on history as something "to be lived up to." Listen, I plead with you, to the words and thoughts of Bruce Catton for the sake of the past, the now, and the future.

E. B. Long
Professor of American Studies
University of Wyoming
formerly Director of Research,
Bruce Catton's *Centennial History
of the Civil War*

PART ONE

A Moving Tide

Except by Violence

The Civil War is probably the most significant single experience in our national existence. It was certainly the biggest tragedy in American history and, at the same time, probably did more to shape our future than any other event.

It settled two things once and for all. In the first place, it determined that there would be one nation, and not two or more, between Canada and Mexico; that there would be unity in the American Republic, that the old theory of State's Rights would wither to the extent that the Federal Government would have the power and the authority to enforce an overall national policy for the entire country.

In addition, the war ended the institution of chattel slavery. That was an institution that the country could not have carried into the twentieth century without suffering a crippling handicap. It is not easy to see how the institution could have been disposed of, except by violence. It had imbedded itself too deeply, not only in the

3

Southern economy and by indirection, in the Northern
economy as well, but in human emotions.

The existence of chattel slavery made it unnecessary
for people to face up to the race problem. Once slavery
was destroyed, and the Civil War did destroy it, the nation was left with a piece of unfinished business. It had
political unity; it had to move ahead and create a moral
and emotional unity as well. Freedom is something for
everybody. There could no longer be grades and distinc-
tions in American citizenship.

The Civil War ended more than a century ago. Nobody
who had firsthand experience of what the American
people were saying or thinking or feeling at that time is
still alive. We take what we know of the war second-
hand and, as it recedes in the distance, as we get farther
and farther away from it, we tend to oversimplify it.
The motives and causes, desires, hatreds, and anxieties
seem clearer now than they did to the people who had to
live through them.

We tend today to write the Civil War off rather
blithely as the great war to end slavery. It was, of
course, the war that did end slavery, but it did not begin
that way at all. It began on a very different basis and, as
a matter of fact, in the month of July 1861, after the
war had gotten well started and both sides were nerving
themselves for a long fight, the Congress of the United
States, with Abraham Lincoln's approval, passed a Resolution saying flatly that the war was not being fought
to interfere with slavery in any way at all. It was being
fought, said this Resolution, solely to restore the Union,
and it would cease when the people who were trying to
break up the Union stopped fighting.

At the same time, the Southern people were equally
clear on the fact that they were not fighting to defend
slavery; they were fighting for their own independence.
They made that as clear as they could through the
Congress and their President, over and over again.

In other words, the two governments that differed on

so many matters were in agreement on that one point—
they weren't fighting over slavery. Yet, of course, they
were. The war was *about* slavery. Slavery had caused it:
If slavery had vanished before 1861, the war simply
would not have taken place. Yet most of the soldiers
who entered the Union army did not really care about
slavery. For that matter, the great majority of soldiers
in the Confederate army did not come from slave-
owning families, never expected to own slaves themselves and to the very end indignantly repelled suggestions that they were fighting in defense of slavery. In the
North it needs to be emphasized that very few of the
soldiers were abolitionists. The majority did not like
black people and for the most part were perfectly willing
for slavery to continue; indeed, many of the older ones
rather hoped that it would, because if it ended, the black
people might flood the North country and take jobs and
farms that otherwise would go to white men.

So one of the great ironies of American history
becomes apparent. The white folk of the United States,
North and South alike, could get along with the black
man as a slave much better than they could get along
with him as a free person; yet slavery in the mid-
nineteenth century was such a fragile institution that it
could not survive unless it was supported by all the
power of the central government, and in a civil war that
support would be withdrawn. Slavery could not conceivably survive a full-scale civil war, yet such a war was
being waged to save it. The very people who wanted
slavery to live were doing precisely the thing that was
sure to kill it.

Deeply buried in the American soul was a seemingly
ineradicable strain of race hatred; of, if that phrase is
too strong, a vast conviction of white superiority that
dominated men's minds at the very moment when they
were taking a baffling and painful road that could lead
only to equality. America's basic charter, the foundation for all that Americans lived by, was the flat
assertion that all men are created equal. Now the nation
was forcing itself to see that "all men" means what it

says. Therein lies the true, eternally baffling mystery of
the Civil War: It did something hardly anyone wanted
done, and it changed the course of American history
forever afterward.

War has a way of compelling men to confront the
realities they try to evade. The Civil War did that with
the institution of slavery. Most people in the North did
not want slavery to exist in their own states, but they felt
very, very little desire to do anything about it in the
South. Even Abraham Lincoln, who is remembered
properly today as the Great Emancipator, did not,
before the war, class himself with the Abolitionists at
all. He once told a Southern friend that there was only
one difference between Northerners like himself and
pro-slavery men in the South. Said Lincoln, "We think
slavery is wrong and ought to be restricted; you think it
is right and ought to be extended. That's the only difference."

The war actually came about because of a very
unrealistic argument—the argument over whether the
Federal Government had the authority and the right to
prohibit slavery in the territories. This was unrealistic
for the simple reason that in the Western territories—
Nebraska, Kansas, New Mexico, Arizona, California—
slavery simply could not exist. This was not the kind of
country in which you could make money running a
large, factory-type farm with gang labor. In New Mexico, for instance, which became part of the Union in
1848, slavery was quite legal, but at the start of the Civil
War it contained only nine slaves. The institution of
slavery simply didn't work there.

Abraham Lincoln believed, and indeed stated, that
the Federal Government did not have the authority to
interfere with slavery in the states; that it was strictly a
state matter. The government in Washington could do
nothing about it, and he did not propose to do anything
about it on the theory that it would, sooner or later, die
in those states where it already existed. However, he did
take a strong stand that there should be no extension of
slavery in the territories.

The Southern leaders paid no attention to the pledge that the Federal Government would not interfere with slavery in the states. Instead, they reacted strongly against the argument that slavery should not be allowed to expand, and the whole, terrible turmoil of the late 1850s which finally led to the war, grew out of this very unrealistic argument over slavery in the territories.

Slavery itself was not a simple institution. Upward of four million black people were held in servitude, most of them as field hands, a sort of gang-labor reserve. They had no liberties. What they got in the way of clothing, food, and housing depended entirely upon either the benevolence or neglect of the people who owned them. They were an indigestible lump, and they endured their lives as slaves as best they could. Indeed, they were a very peace-loving people. They were not vengeful. They remained so quiet, as a matter of fact, that a great many people in both sections of the country took it for granted that they were more or less content with their lot. Now and then, to be sure, the curtain would be drawn aside and a glimpse of the truth would appear. The Nat Turner Rebellion, for instance, long before the Civil War, was a grim example of the hatreds and passions that lay under the surface.

Another point, which probably accounts for much of their docility under slavery, is the simple fact that the more energetic forward-looking, independent slaves were drained off by the institution of the underground railroad. They were the ones who ran away. They got to the Northern states or all the way to Canada, taking with them the intelligence, the drive, the eagerness that might have made them leaders of a slave revolt.

So, for years, by and large, the slave population of the South seemed quite placid and the people of the South, whose institutions were based on slavery, felt relatively secure.

Slavery, as it existed in the South in 1860, varied a great deal from state to state. In the Northern slave states, like Kentucky, Maryland, and Virginia, slavery was a fairly mild institution. The slaves were pretty well

taken care of. Old Massa was kindly; they got along
with him. A great many of them seemed not too unhappy with their lot. Where slavery was really hard,
where it bore down on them, was in the Deep South
along the Gulf Coast, in the great cotton states. A slave
in the Northern belt of slave states who was unruly and
hard to get along with and talked back to Old Massa
would be threatened with, "We'll sell you down the
river." And, if he didn't watch his step, he *was* sold
down the river, which meant that he got sold down to
Louisiana or Mississippi or Alabama or Texas. That
was where the slave worked until he dropped, and was
finally worked to death; that was where Simon Legree,
of *Uncle Tom's Cabin*, lived. Getting "sold down the
river" was a very real and terrible threat in those days.

The people in the North were greatly influenced by
Uncle Tom's Cabin and took their impression of slavery
from the picture it painted of the down-river slave life,
where the slave was part of a great gang-labor setup,
was worked from dawn to dusk, was flogged un-
mercifully when he misbehaved, and finally worked
himself to death for no personal gain.

The Curtain Drawn Aside

When the Republicans won in the 1860 election, and Abraham Lincoln was the President-elect, the leaders of the Cotton Belt in the Deep South knew perfectly well that although he was not an Abolitionist and had never advocated the destruction of slavery in the states, slavery was not safe with him in the White House. They knew the tide was going to turn with a President and a dominant political party in Washington committed to the checking of slavery in the territories. They knew that if slavery was no longer able to expand, it eventually would have to die.

If the Southerners did not feel that they were going to war to defend slavery, they did have a deep feeling that the race question that would confront them if slavery were abolished was more than they could handle. They had been brought up, despite the quietness of their slave population, to suspect that under the surface dangerous violence lurked. The example of Santo Domingo, where the slaves rose in revolt and massacred all the white

people they could get their hands on, was something
they never forgot. The Nat Turner Rebellion had
pointed in that direction. A few other outbreaks in the
South seemed to point the same way. And most Southerners frankly confessed that they did not see how the
two races could get along together if the institution of
slavery were removed. If the Southerners were not fighting to preserve slavery, then they were at least fighting
to preserve a situation in which they did not have to be
afraid of a sudden, violent uprising by the slave population.

What made John Brown, for instance, such a hated
character in the South, was the fact that his strange
abortive raid at Harpers Ferry was designed as a step to
stir up a slave rebellion. If it had succeeded, it would undoubtedly have gotten out of hand. Brown was the man
to start something like that; not the man to control it.
Fortunately, it did not succeed and the country was
spared what would have been a very tragic, bloody experience. But the fact that such a tragic, bloody experience seemed to lie below the surface of their lives
was a frightening thing to the people of the South and
helped persuade a great many that safety, for them, lay
in getting out of the Union.

The black man in the North was not a slave, but he
was very definitely not merely a second-class citizen, but
a third- or fourth-class citizen. He had few rights, practically no privileges, and no social standing whatever. In
general, the poorest jobs, the lowest wages, and the
worst housing were reserved for him. In some cases, indeed, it was possible to argue that some slaves in the
South might be better off than black people were in the
North, strictly from the standpoint of food, clothing,
housing, and general treatment. Of course, that argument missed the point because, above everything else,
the slave wanted his freedom, and he was willing to pay
a high price for it; and he did. The rest of the country
paid an equal price to get it for him.

When the war began and Northern armies moved
down into the South, the soldiers in the Northern armies

discovered that the black men who were all around them
were somehow on their side. The soldiers felt that they
were in a foreign country, simply because slavery did
exist there. They passed the plantations with their slave
quarters behind the big house and the work gangs out in
the field. This was not like life in Ohio or Pennsylvania
or Vermont. This was foreign; it was different. The
people here were enemies and yet, somehow, these black
folk were friendly. If a soldier was lost from his unit, or
had straggled after a battle and did not know where he
was or how to get back, it was the black people who
would help him. They would give him something to eat,
they would put him on the road, they would help him
dodge the Confederate patrols; they were always on his
side. Furthermore, they soon clustered around the
camps and the Northern soldier began to realize that
there was something wrong with the argument that the
slaves were contented with their lot.

At first the Federal Government took the position
that the army must not harbor fugitive slaves. In fact, it
was officially stated that the army as a whole would
have nothing to do with slavery. That, of course, was
like saying that the army would have nothing to do with
the weather. It was fighting the war where slavery was,
and it was bound to have something to do with it even if
it tried its best not to.

Ben Butler, an army officer from Boston, came up
with an ingenious theory in response to the Federal
Government's decree. He was in command of troops
down near Norfolk, Virginia, in the early part of the
war, and a great many slaves flocked around his camp
seeking refuge. Butler brought up the point that under
the laws of war and under the United States War
Department regulations, he or any other Union officer
was authorized to seize contraband of war; that is,
property that the Confederate army was using in its
fight for independence. He could seize clothing or ammunition that came into his possession. He could seize
horses and livestock that were intended for army use.
He could, of course, seize guns or ammunition. He

could seize supplies of any kind that were helping the
Confederate army in its fight. Butler remarked that, as
far as he could see, slaves were property. That, indeed,
was the argument of all Southerners. If they were property and if they were being used to aid the Rebel army,
then, said Butler, they were contraband of war and the
Northern army could seize them and at least deprive
their Southern masters of their use.

In the beginning, this reasoning applied only to slaves
who traveled with the Confederate army as teamsters, as
diggers of fortifications, as camp servants. The War
Department approved of Butler's ingenious argument
and agreed that such slaves could be, and were, taken
away from their owners.

But the theory spread very rapidly beyond that. The
War Department began to realize that although the
slaves might not be used by the army at all, although
they might not ever see a Confederate soldier, their
presence in the field or in the shops that used slave labor
was a direct asset to the embattled Confederacy. The
South lived on the food they raised, it clothed itself in
the cotton they grew, its entire economy rested on the
institution of slavery; and Northern generals in the
South, to say nothing of private soldiers, before long
began to see that anything that weakened the institution
of slavery weakened the Confederate army. To strike at
the army, you struck at the economy that supported it.
It was then a slightly new theory as far as formal warfare was concerned, but today is embodied in the
bombing raids all countries carry out in an effort to
destroy factories, railroad lines, warehouses, anything
that the opposing economy needs.

So the Northern armies moving down into the South
began to dismantle the institution of slavery, not
because they had anything against it, not because the
men particularly liked black people, but simply because
the institution was there and was obviously supporting
the government and the army that were making war
against the Federal Union.

Wherever a Union army went, slaves were taken away

from their masters. Butler, again, pointed to the odd situation that now developed. He said, in effect, that these slaves no longer belonged to their masters because they had been working in support of the Rebellion and we have declared them dislodged, and they are now with our army; we are supporting them. Now, if they don't belong to their old masters, whom do they belong to? In effect, Butler said, they don't belong to me; I don't want them. They don't belong to the Northern government because the Northern government doesn't want them; it has nothing in its law that empowers it to own slaves. If they don't belong to their old masters and don't belong to the army and don't belong to the government, then, said Butler, it must be that they are free people. This was a view, however, that the people in the North were not quite ready to accept. They went along for a long time trying to pretend that they were simply seizing contraband of war and doing their best to make use of the workers who came within their lines; and they did use them quite a bit, particularly in the western theater, where they got more of them. In Tennessee, northern Mississippi, Missouri, Arkansas they set up great camps to accommodate fugitive slaves. These camps were run with the best intentions, but with inadequate supplies and very poor management, they resembled present-day concentration camps more than we like to think about. Some of these camps were extremely bad places, and there are cases on record of fugitive slaves who, after a few weeks in one, asked if they could not go back to their old masters; they had it better on the plantations.

But, most did not feel that way, and, by and large, the camps did support them, feed them, clothe them, and give them some kind of hope for a better life ahead.

By the late summer of 1862, Abraham Lincoln concluded that it was time to take the final step to proclaim freedom for the slaves, but he was faced with the fact that both Northerners and Southerners had been

agreeing for many years that the Federal Government
had no control over slavery and that it was a matter for
the states. The Federal Government therefore did not
have the power to free the slaves, nor did the President
himself. So Lincoln worked out a clever solution. The
war powers of the President, he pointed out, are almost
unlimited. He is in command of the Army and the
Navy, and subject to ratification by Congress, he can do
just about anything that he thinks needs to be done to
win a war. We have seen that same argument used in our
own time, and it is an inescapable part of the American
system. Lincoln concluded that he could proclaim
freedom for the slaves as a war measure, and that accounts for the odd shape that the Emancipation
Proclamation took. It proclaimed freedom for the
slaves in precisely those areas where the government
could not enforce freedom; that is, the Deep South,
where its armies had not as yet obtained control.

In the border states, Kentucky, Missouri, and Maryland, which had remained with the Union, the Emancipation Proclamation *specifically* had no effect. In such
states as Tennessee and Virginia the Proclamation applied only to the areas that were still in rebellion, and
not to the ones that had been pacified.

In other words, it proclaimed freedom from slavery
where the government could not enforce the Proclamation and left it untouched in the areas where it could. It
seems at this distance an extremely weak, milk-and-
water sort of Proclamation, and on the face of it, it is.
And yet it was one of the most powerful, important,
consequential proclamations any American President
ever issued.

We should not be surprised that that was the case.
The word "freedom" is a dangerous word. It is like
phosphorus; you take it out in the open air, and it
ignites; you can't toss it about carelessly. Much earlier,
four score and seven years earlier, the American
colonists had put the word "freedom" into their
statement of what they were fighting for. By doing it,
they turned an armed protest into a revolution. They

created a new nation and turned loose in the world a divine unrest whose end is not yet seen.

Lincoln did the same thing in 1862 when he confronted four million black slaves and, with however many provisos and qualifications, went on to say that these people would be then henceforward and forever free. The slaves took him very seriously. They did not have access to newspapers, and most of them couldn't have read them if they had. They were locked away, far behind the army, and yet they knew almost instantaneously that the President of the United States was saying that they were going to be free. From that moment on, slavery was doomed.

General William T. Sherman, who was far from being an Abolitionist, remarked in 1863 that "the whole army of the United States could not restore the institution of slavery in the South; they can't get back their slaves, any more than they can get back their dead grandfathers; it is dead." And Sherman was quite right.

The Northern armies, which had been dismantling the institution wherever they went, continued to do so with something definite in mind now. They weren't just trying to take away armed servants from the Confederate army. It occurred to various people in the North, starting with the President and Secretary of War, that if these black people were free and if the army was going south in order to free them, then possibly some of them could join the army themselves and do some fighting for this freedom.

It took the old line army a little while to get used to this idea. The regular army officers had very little regard for it, and a great many of the rank and file also preferred not to see the colored man in an army uniform.

But the idea had a logic of its own. Most of the soldiers—the private soldiers—who had started by saying that they didn't want black men in uniform began to reason that if a hundred thousand black men went out to fight, they might do some fighting which would otherwise have to be done by one hundred

thousand white men. As they said, rather crudely, "A
black man can stop a bullet just as well as a white man."
The work of recruiting black troops began in 1863 and
was carried on with great vigor.

Yet, as one might suppose, the treatment the black
man got after he enlisted varied greatly from place to
place. In a great number of cases, white officers and
troops simply assumed that these black troops who were
joining them were a kind of labor gang that could repair
roads and dig trenches and pull wagons out of swamps,
but they weren't really to be counted on as soldiers. On
the other hand, there were places where an honest effort
was made to treat the black men as soldiers and use
them as such. During the siege of Vicksburg, for instance, a Confederate army came out of the Southwest
and attacked the Union lines along the Mississippi River
a little upstream from Vicksburg. As it turned out, the
principal defenders there were a few black regiments,
newly enlisted. They fell into line, fought, repelled the
assault and, according to U. S. Grant, who was a fairly
good judge of such matters, acquitted themselves very
well indeed. The episode seemed to prove that the black
man could be, and would be, if permitted, a good
soldier.

In the East, also, the proof began to appear. When
the Union army made its great attack overland at
Charleston and tried to capture Battery Wagner, which
was the principal strong point defending this Southern
city, two black regiments, the 54th and 55th Massa-
chusetts, spearheaded the assault. The assault should
not have been made at all because the battery was too
strong to be carried, and the 54th and 55th, like some of
the white regiments that joined in it, were very badly
shot up. But, there again, the black man had proved
that when given the chance he was a soldier as good as
any other, and was quite as well able to go where the
bullets were flying.

In the siege of Petersburg black soldiers were used
quite prominently. Again, they were thrown into a

hopeless venture at the great Battle of the Crater and suffered very heavy casualties. But they were used, and they acquitted themselves well. They were also put into action toward the closing part of the war in the force that lay siege to Richmond itself.

An odd thing comes out in the connection. The Union officer who was in charge of the section of the army directly facing Richmond was a man named Godfrey Weitzel. He had served in New Orleans under Ben Butler in early 1863 and had objected vigorously when he was placed in command of certain black regiments which had just been raised. He did not believe in black troops; he said he couldn't handle them, he didn't want them. Two years later, after Grant broke Lee's lines at the Battle of Five Forks and compelled the Confederate army to retreat from Petersburg and then from Richmond, Godfrey Weitzel led the first Union troops into Richmond; more than half of them were black regiments. Apparently, the General found out that he could handle black troops, after all.

The story of slavery and the men who had been slaves does not end when the war ended. The most tragic part of it, I think, comes later, when the slow tragic process of disillusionment came to the men and women who had been brought out of slavery, when they began to see that doors were still closed to them, that they were not masters of their own fate appreciably more than they had been before. There was, in short, a catch to freedom.

For many, many years, for generations, America's black people tried with great patience and in a most orderly way to work their way out of the great weight of discrimination which was their heritage from the days of slavery. The problem has not yet been entirely solved. It is on the road to solution, but it will be a long process. We are still stuck with the heritage that came down to us from the Civil War, white and black alike. The Civil War proclaimed freedom and made freedom good, on paper at least. It proclaimed national unity, and made that good. Ever since then, the American people have had a great commitment to themselves and to society as a whole.

It is up to them, up to us—you and me and all of us—to prove that a free society like ours can be a unit and can extend freedom to all of its members—a classless society, if you like, not because all men are of equal ability, since, obviously, they are not, but because they are all of equal rights and all are disposed to respect one another's rights. We are dedicated to a society in which one man's fate affects the fate of all the rest, in which your freedom and my freedom depend on the freedom of less-fortunate people. We defend our own freedom by defending theirs, by seeing to it that they have the chance to defend theirs. That is our heritage from the Civil War.

If we live up to it, and I think in the course of time, we will, it will be worth everything we paid for it—the 600,000 lives that were offered up, the infinity of pain and suffering endured by people of both sides. What we have today was bought by them.

Throwing Its Coils

The odd thing about the beginning of the war was that nobody had made any plans whatever. The general theory, both North and South, seemed to be that this would be a short war. Each side, of course, expected to win it and to win it quickly. But there were no plans; there was no strategic grasp of the problem at all. For the Union army there would be a quick march down to Richmond, and that would be it.

The exception, of course, was General Winfield Scott, the ranking General in the United States Army. He was an old man and his health was not good. It was so bad, in fact, that he couldn't get on a horse, and couldn't even think of campaigning in the field. But he, nevertheless, was in command of the United States Army. He was an extremely good soldier, very conscientious, and he brought forth a plan for defeating the Southern Confederacy.

According to Scott, the Navy should throw a tight blockade all up and down the Confederate coast. Inland, detachments of the Army should blockade roads leading north and south. Then there should be a major offensive thrust down the valley of the Mississippi River to split off that part of the Confederacy lying west of the Mississippi. This would be followed by other thrusts: south through Tennessee and into Georgia, east from New Orleans into southern Alabama and, of course, south from Washington, through Richmond, into the Carolinas.

As Scott laid this out he knew it was going to take a good deal of time. In the first place, the armies had to be raised and equipped and trained. The Navy, which was going to do this blockading, had to be increased. It was going to be a slow process, and in place of the two or three months' war that everybody was talking about, Scott was looking ahead to a war that would take two or three years, or even longer.

His idea was not particularly popular with the country at large. The press fastened on to it the epithet "The Anaconda Plan," evoking the image of that great South American serpent, the anaconda, which like a boa constrictor throws its coils around the victim and slowly immobilizes him. There was something too slow, almost passive, about this plan to strike the fancy of the people up north, both in the government and out of it. They wanted to move fast, and Scott was very widely derided for bringing such an idea forward.

As it worked out, something very much like the Anaconda Plan was the plan the North finally followed. It was the plan that finally won the war. The name itself had been dropped and Scott's connection with it had been, more or less, forgotten; but the plan that he brought forth in the summer of 1861 was essentially the plan through which the North won the war.

It had to begin with the blockade, and it was at this point that Abraham Lincoln apparently learned a little something about international law. When drafting the proclamation of the blockade of the Southern ports he used the wrong language, without in the least meaning to, and came very close to legally recognizing the

Southern Confederacy. You don't blockade the ports of
your own nation. In case of insurrection or civil dis-
order of any kind, you issue a proclamation closing the
ports; the effects are much the same, but the language is
very different.

In any case, tne Federal navy got busy. It was not a
large, strong force at the time, but the Confederacy had
no navy whatever and so its task was somewhat simpler.
Furthermore, although the Southern Confederacy had a
seacoast hundreds and hundreds of miles in length,
there were not more than half a dozen important ports
that needed to be blockaded. Regular full-fledged warships were not needed to enforce the blockade, because
the blockaders were simply trying to keep unarmed merchant ships from coming in or going out. As a result,
almost anything that could float and carry a gun could
serve as a warship on blockade.

In one way or another, by buying merchant ships and
converting them into warships, and by hastily building a
large number of gunboats (they called them ''ninety-day
gunboats'' because it took just ninety days from the moment the contract was signed until the boats were ready
for use), the navy fairly soon got a more or less bus-
inesslike blockade into operation. It was not, of course,
as effective in the first year or two as it became later.
But the simple fact that it existed had quite an effect on
the merchant ship owners in England and France. It
might be true that the odds that they could get a ship full
of supplies through the blockade were, at that time,
quite good. But, at the same time, there was also a
chance of complete failure. The merchants might very
well lose ship and cargo altogether. So a number of
them refused to try to send goods to the Confederacy,
simply because a blockade existed on paper.

This was important for it kept the Confederacy from
getting the supplies it needed. Because the Confederacy
was not a manufacturing country it had to import a
great number of things from Europe; guns, gunpowder,
cannon, uniforms, all the things that an army has to
have.

The Confederacy needed not only to import a great deal of material, they also had to send out exports to pay for the imported goods; as a new nation which had not established itself yet, the Confederacy's credit in the European market was extremely poor.

The one export that the Confederacy had which was greatly desired by Europe was cotton. Cotton, the Southerners used to boast, was king. Indeed, the impetus toward secession early in 1861 owed a great deal to the general belief that England and France, which used much cotton in their textile mills, simply would not put up with a stoppage of cotton exports from the South. In the early months, the Confederate government even disapproved of sending cotton abroad on the grounds that this would put increased pressure on England and France to intervene on their behalf. This strategy did not last very long, however. It became altogether too obvious that the Confederacy had to get cotton overseas in order to buy the things it had to have to fight the war.

When cotton exports were resumed, they had to be made largely in British and French ships simply because the Southern states did not, in the 1860s, have very much in the way of a merchant marine. American goods were carried pretty largely by ships owned in the North. So when the Confederacy became isolated, it had to rely on the blockade runners. These were fast ships, cheaply built, designed to slip in and out of Southern ports as quickly as possible. Afterwards, they would go to depots in the Bahamas or Bermuda or Cuba where the goods could be transferred to sturdier craft to cross the ocean. Since the ships were not very expensive to build and the profits that could be made by running the blockade were great, a ship could be paid for in one or two round trips. So the blockade runners went into business, and the United States Navy did its best to catch up with them.

There was one point that everybody expected would be important, but turned out not to be, and that was the use of privateers. In all earlier wars at sea, a blockaded nation would make great use of privateers. We did in the War of 1812 when we fought the British. The privateer was a private shipowner who got a license from his government to go hunting. He was an ocean cruiser under private ownership who could swarm over enemy shipping lanes on his own and was entitled to keep or sell any ships or cargos he captured. Naturally, this created a great deal of enthusiasm for privateering among shipowners in the blockaded country. The Confederacy was expected to use a great many privateers; it did, in fact, use a few, but gave it up before long and the privateer was never an important factor in the Civil War.

The reason for this was that the Confederacy relied on at least a friendly attitude on the part of Great Britain. They hoped that eventually Great Britain would take their side and intervene, the way France did in the Revolutionary War. But, failing that, they at least wanted a benevolent neutrality, so to speak, and the one thing the British government did not want to see, then or at any other time, was a growth of privateering. As the greatest naval power in the world and the greatest merchant shipping nation, the British detested the idea of privateering. It had cost them an enormous sum in the War of 1812; it had cost them even more in the wars with Napoleon, and they never wanted to hear of privateers again. They would do nothing to encourage it, and would obviously not be very friendly toward a country that indulged in privateering. The North, trying to enforce its blockade, and well aware that there was a great deal of sentiment in England and France in favor of the Southern Confederacy, had to make it clear to London and Paris, without actually seeming to seek trouble, that any overt act on the part of a foreign government in support of the Southern Confederacy would result in war.

William H. Seward, the Secretary of State in Lincoln's cabinet, had realized this from the beginning. Seward was in a somewhat difficult position when the war began. He had been the leading Republican candidate for the Presidency and his defeat by Abraham

Lincoln at the Chicago Convention was something of an
upset, and something to which Seward had some difficulty adjusting himself. When the Lincoln administration took office, Secretary Seward was quite firmly of
the opinion that it was up to him to run the country. He
was only Secretary of State, of course, but the Secretary
of State was supposed to be the top man in the cabinet.
Mr. Seward believed that Mr. Lincoln was quite in-
capable of being a good executive and that Lincoln
should sit back and, like the King of England, reign but
not rule; that he should be a figurehead while the administration should be run by the Secretary of State,
namely, Mr. Seward.

One of Seward's ideas, when war with the Confederacy became imminent, was that if the United States
got into a good, severe quarrel with a traditional enemy
like England, the people of the South would forget their
enthusiasm for independence and would rally around
the flag. A war with England, in other words, would
reunite the country, and get us out of the necessity of
having to subdue the Southern states.

Seward was quite ready to take a menacing attitude
toward the British; in fact, he was a little too ready.
Several weeks after the administration had taken office,
before the firing on Fort Sumter actually opened the
shooting war, Seward sent Mr. Lincoln a very strange
memorandum. In it he asserted that although the administration had already been in office for several
weeks, it had no policy, it was doing nothing, and that
someone had to take charge and shape the country's
policy so that people would know what they were trying
to do. He suggested that harsh words be dispatched to
both British and French governments.

This memorandum did not meet with a warm recep-
tion from Abraham Lincoln. He never said anything
about it in public. Instead, he simply wrote Mr. Seward
a little note in reply (whether he in fact sent the note is
not clear) pointing out that the country did have a policy
and that the policy firmly stated that the government
was not going to stand for secession, and that it would

retain its forts and others bits of property in the Southern states. This policy, Mr. Lincoln wrote, was perfectly clear; it had been voiced in his Inaugural Address and never been retreated from; he was quite unable to see, he said, how stirring up a quarrel in Europe would help us solve our quarrel at home, and he added that it was very clear to him that whatever was done, he would be the one to do it, and he would expect from his Secretary of State, as from his other cabinet members, loyal support and assistance.

You have to say one thing for Seward. He had tried. He quickly learned that Lincoln was not going to have any of this, and he adjusted himself with remarkable speed to become a good, loyal member of the administration family. As the war years passed, Seward became really quite close to Abraham Lincoln in a personal sense. They got along fine, once Lincoln had made it clear just who was going to be boss.

At this point in 1861, the war got rolling with a blockade, which would take a year or two to become fully effective, with large armies being organized, equipped, and trained, and finally with moves of invasion much like the ones Winfield Scott had suggested. Scott himself was not around long to direct things. As the summer of 1861 wore away, it became apparent that the old man simply wasn't physically up to it. In addition, the new young General, George B. McClellan, who had been called in to take charge of the Army of the Potomac, looked on General Scott as a hindrance and wanted him out of there. McClellan got a good deal of support for this attitude because the Anaconda Plan had been so unpopular. McClellan was seen as the bright young man from the West Virginia mountains who had done beautifully with a brief campaign there and who obviously had the spirit that would lead to victory. So in the middle of the fall of 1861, General Scott was relieved from command and retired to his home, and General McClellan moved to Washington to become General-in-Chief of all the Union armies. In addition to being in command of all the armies, he assumed

personal command of the Army of the Potomac, the
army that was both Washington's defender and the
assailant of the Confederate capital at Richmond.

Since those days, it has been remarked that the defense of Washington handicapped Union strategy and
that the Union probably would have been better off if
its capital city had been at some more remote place like
Philadelphia or New York where it would not have been
such a tempting target for Confederate armies. The difficulty with that was that the United States was not, at
that time, fighting a foreign war; it was fighting a civil
war, and above everything, it had to demonstrate to its
own people and to the people in Europe that it was capable of sustaining itself. Whatever it did, it did not
dare evacuate Washington. It had to hold Washington
at all costs, from the beginning of the war right down to
the end. That put a strategic problem on the shoulders
of the generals who were in charge of the Union army,
but the problem was quite unavoidable.

In the early spring of 1862 when McClellan took his
army down to Hampton Roads and started moving up
the Virginia peninsula toward Richmond, he was badly
handicapped because Lincoln and Secretary of War
Stanton insisted that he keep forty or fifty thousand
troops in the vicinity of Washington so that it would be
impossible for a sudden Confederate offensive to capture the capital city. McClellan objected to this very bitterly; he became estranged from Secretary Stanton and
eventually from President Lincoln. He considered that
they had put an impossible handicap on him and, when
his great campaign to capture Richmond failed in the
spring of 1862, forcing him to take refuge down the
James River and call for reinforcements, he insisted that
the chief trouble was the fact that the government in
Washington had interfered with him.

The trouble, however, was that the government had
no choice. The one way it was sure to lose the war
quickly would be to lose the capital city; that would
convince everybody—in London, in Paris, in Richmond, and in the United States as well—that the United

States Government was quite unable to put down what it called a mere rebellion. Whether McClellan liked it or not, Lincoln and Stanton had to hold a certain number of troops in hand to keep Washington safe. They did that throughout the war, and every Union General in the East who moved out against Robert E. Lee moved under that handicap. Finally, in 1864 they found a man named Grant who was able to operate in spite of handicaps. But to everybody else, it proved a profound problem.

A Strong President

Being President of the United States in wartime is, of course, an overwhelming job. The President has to be a military strategist because he is, in the long run, the Commander in Chief of the country's armed forces. He also has to be enough of an economist and a financier to see to it that proper steps are taken to keep the country's economy running and to keep its currency reasonably stable. On top of everything else, he has to be what he was elected to be in the first place. That is, a political leader, a politician who can work through other politicians.

Lincoln developed into one of the most canny politicians this country has seen. He worked largely through his Cabinet, which included some of the men who had run against him in the 1860 Republican Presidential Nomination Campaign. Secretary of State Seward, as noted earlier, was bitterly disappointed when he was beaten by this dark horse from Illinois. But Seward was probably the man who wound up feeling the

most affection for Lincoln and the man with whom Lincoln felt most at ease. It was Seward who gave Lincoln
the one piece of advice about the Emancipation
Proclamation that Lincoln was willing to accept;
namely, that it could not be issued until the Union
armies had won a substantial victory. Lincoln harkened
to that, put the Proclamation away, and brought it out
only after the Battle of Antietam.

He was close to his Secretary of State all through the
war, and significantly enough, on the night that Booth
shot Lincoln at Ford's Theatre, one of Booth's co-
conspirators forced his way into Seward's house and
tried to kill him with a dagger. Seward survived, of
course, and served on for some time as Secretary of
State. (It was under Seward that the United States
bought Alaska from Russia, and for quite a while when
the ordinary citizen could not see that there was any particular use in owning Alaska, this territory was known
as Seward's Folly.)

The other most recognizable member of Lincoln's
Cabinet was Edwin M. Stanton, who became Secretary
of War early in 1862. After the war, Stanton was known
as a Republican Radical. He did not come into the
Cabinet with that reputation; on the contrary, he had
served briefly in President Buchanan's Cabinet and had
been a Democrat. When Lincoln appointed him to the
War Department it was generally assumed that here was
a case where Lincoln was reaching into the opposition
party and taking a Democrat for an important job.

Stanton was a brusque, rather dictatorial man. He
scared the daylights out of army officers who had to
come to see him. He would bark at them, storm at them,
snarl at them, threaten them openly with breaking them
down to enlisted man's status or firing them out of the
service altogether. He was, all in all, a tough man to get
along with. For quite a while, he rather despaired of
President Lincoln. Lincoln's habit of cracking jokes
repelled Stanton; he did not have a sense of humor
anywhere about his person.

Once or twice when President Lincoln would open a

Cabinet meeting by reading a chapter or two from one of the popular humorists of the day, like Josh Billings or Artemus Ward, Stanton could hardly contain his indignation. The idea that the President of the United States, who had important business to take care of, would spend five minutes relaxing in laughter was more than Stanton could endure. Yet as the war wore on, Lincoln and Stanton worked closely together. Stanton had many of the qualities Lincoln needed. Lincoln, on the other hand, had the ability to control Stanton's occasionally violent, dictatorial tendencies and to put his tremendous energy to use without letting his quirks spoil everything. Lincoln, once or twice, humorously remarked that the Secretary of War was running the war and that the President had no influence at all in the War Department. It was actually very clear, particularly toward the end of the war, that Lincoln was the man in charge and Stanton was the Executive Officer.

After Lincoln died in the rooming house across the street from Ford's Theatre, Stanton, reflecting on all that had happened, said, "There lies the greatest master of men that ever lived." It was testimony from an expert.

Through those two men, then, Lincoln ran the country during the Civil War. He had other assistants, of course. His Secretary of the Navy, Gideon Welles of Connecticut, was an extremely useful person. Welles had been in politics for many years, an old Andrew Jackson Democrat. A great many people considered him a mildly comic figure. He had abundant, bushy, white whiskers and because he was totally bald, he wore a wig—but it was a bushy wig of a different color than his whiskers. He was irascible, petulant, and suspicious. He disliked Stanton very much, and liked Seward only a little better. He turned out to be a first-rate Secretary of the Navy, and before the war was over, people could see that. Lincoln never had to worry too much about what the Navy was doing and he never had to worry in the least about Gideon Welles' loyalty to him and to the Union cause.

For the most part, the other members of the Cabinet are merely names today. The one exception is Secretary of the Treasury Simon P. Chase. It's a little hard, at this distance, to warm up to Chase. He was a man convinced of his own rightness; he had no more sense of humor than had Stanton; he tended to be a little sanctimonious; and he was convinced, down to the summer of 1864 at least, that he was destined to replace Lincoln in the White House. As a matter of fact, he campaigned against Lincoln quite vigorously in the early part of 1864 until finally he was compelled to see that the people in the country were not in the least likely to elect him to Mr. Lincoln's place.

Lincoln bore him no hard feelings. Indeed, he appointed him Chief Justice of the United States before the year was out, and Chase served with distinction.

These were the men through whom Lincoln worked at his job of politics. If you look back at the past, you're likely to find that all of the note-worthy Presidents, the Presidents who have done the most, were expert politicians. A President has to start with politics. Lincoln certainly did.

You hear a great deal of talk these days about the merits or demerits of having a strong Presidency. Probably there is a good deal to be said on both sides, but one thing is quite certain. If there had not been a strong Presidency and a strong President to go with it in 1861, the country unquestionably would have broken apart. Congress was not in session when the firing on Fort Sumter began. That firing, of course, inaugurated the war. But Congress was not present to declare war, to appropriate money, to do any of the things that a government has to do when it wages war.

Lincoln promptly called a special session but stipulated that it should meet three months later. For three months, in other words, the President, and he alone, was the government. It was the President who decided that the firing on Fort Sumter would be treated

as an act of war and that the government would make
war in order to preserve the Union. He committed the
country to raising a large army and to expanding the
navy. He made commitments that Congress, when it
finally met, could do nothing but endorse.

He also took an even stronger step in connection with
the attempt to move Federal troops through the city of
Baltimore, where pro-Confederate sentiment ran very
high. Baltimore, in fact, was looked upon in some
quarters as a secessionist city, although the state of
Maryland never left the Union. But there were elements
in Baltimore, including members of the city government, that were very much opposed to any attempts to
coerce the South, did not want to see the Federal
Government making war on the South, and did everything they could to hamper the war program.

Lincoln simply issued an order suspending the
privilege of the Writ of Habeas Corpus in and around
Baltimore. He authorized the Federal Army Commander there to take such steps as seemed necessary to
him to preserve order and enable the Government to get
on with the war. These steps included making a large
number of strictly arbitrary arrests, arrests which ordinarily could not be made unless someone had sufficient evidence to go to a Grand Jury for an indictment.
City officials were thrown into jail and leading men of
various ranks were similarly arrested and locked up with
no real charges against any of them except the very
vague and general one that they were hampering the war
effort.

It is precisely that sort of thing that the Constitution
was set up to prevent. Clause 2, Section 9, Article I,
guarantees every citizen the protection of the Writ of
Habeas Corpus, under which a court can compel the
authorities to either release a man who has been arrested
or to file formal charges against him in the regular way
and make them stick in the ordinary courts of law.

The Constitution does say that this Writ may not be
suspended *except* in case of insurrection or invasion. It
does not say who is authorized to suspend it in such

cases. Lincoln simply went ahead on the theory that the President did. He came under wide criticism for this, and to this day the argument still rages. But he succeeded in neutralizing the opposition from secessionist forces.

The government was able to move troops through Baltimore. The attempt to cut Washington off from the rest of the North failed. The state of Maryland was kept in the Union, largely because the people who wanted to take it out of the Union were thrown into jail. In the end, the war effort went smoothly, and in the end also, the people who had been jailed were released.

But, meanwhile, the act had been taken. When Congress finally convened in July, it could do nothing but sign the blank check that Mr. Lincoln had made out, endorse all of the things he had done, and make legal, by its own enactment, various things that technically had been illegal to that moment.

The strong Presidency, in other words, saved the Union in the first few months of the war. There simply is no question about it. A President who had sat back and felt that he could do nothing unless and until he had a mandate from the proper authorities would have seen the Union break into fragments. It almost did, anyway. Only a very strong and determined man kept the break from becoming permanent.

It May Be Forever

When it became obvious that there was going to be a shooting war between the North and the South, there were days of immense personal conflict to a great many regular army officers. Among them, of course, was Robert E. Lee, who was one of the most famous officers in the army and to whom Winfield Scott offered top command of the Union army. Lee took a day or two to meditate over this. As a professional army officer, naturally, this was the greatest opportunity that could be offered him—not the sort of thing a man turns down lightly. But he finally refused it on the grounds that he was, after all, a loyal son of Virginia. We don't have that sort of loyalty to homeland these days, but they did then. Lee had it as did a great many other man. Lee had to go with his state, and so turned down the promotion and became a General in the Confederate army.

Other officers on lower levels had the same problem. There was a very poignant incident that occurred in what was then the little country town of Los Angeles. In an army fort near the town, one night in the spring, a farewell party in the officers' quarters was given for some of the officers who were resigning their commissions to go South, as Lee had done. Others were staying in the Union army. One of the latter was a Captain named Winfield Scott Hancock. During the course of the evening, an old friend, Captain Lewis Armistead, came to him. With tears in his eyes, Armistead took Hancock's hand and gripped it, saying, "Hancock, you'll never know what this is costing me, but good-bye, good-bye."

As they were saying good-bye, a woman who was present, the wife of one of the officers, sat at the piano and sang that haunting tune "Kathleen Mavourneen"—"When will we see each other; it may be for years and it may be forever."

Armistead went to Richmond; Hancock to Washington. In July of 1863, these two old friends who had not seen each other since that spring evening in Los Angeles crossed paths at the Battle of Gettysburg. Hancock was in charge of the Union line on Cemetery Ridge around that famous landmark, the "little clump of trees." Pickett's Charge was heroically moving forward, and at the spearhead of it was a man who carried his felt hat on the point of his sword and waved it high over his head so that his soldiers could see it; the man was General Lewis Armistead. As the Confederates reached the Union line and broke into the middle of it, Hancock was shot down with a wound in his thigh.

Armistead reached a battery in the center of Hancock's line, placed his hand on the muzzle of one of the cannons, waved that hat on the point of his sword, and then was shot. He lived just long enough to ask the officers who tried to pick him up and tend him to give his love to General Hancock. It was that kind of war.

PART TWO

Life in the Army

———————————

Country Boys

In the Civil War, the common soldiers of both sides were the same sort of people; untrained and untaught young men, mostly from the country. There weren't many cities then, and they weren't very large, so the average soldier generally came from either a farm or from some very small town or rural area. He had never been anywhere; he was completely unsophisticated. He joined up because he wanted to, because his patriotism had been aroused. The bands were playing, the recruiting officers were making speeches, so he got stirred up and enlisted. Sometimes, he was not altogether dry behind the ears.

When the boy joined the army he would, of course, be issued clothing. He would get his uniform—pants, coat, shoes, and underwear. In the frontier regions, the quartermasters discovered that quite a lot of these young men picked up the underwear and looked at it and said, ''What is this?'' They had never seen any before. They hadn't worn it back home. Well, they

caught on. They were fresh out of the back woods, most
of them.

The boys from the country and the very small towns
seemed to have made better soldiers than the boys from
the cities. In the North, for instance, the boys from the
rural areas, and especially from the Middle West, which
they then called the Northwest, were a little tougher
than the boys from the big cities. They could stand
more, they were more self-reliant, perhaps they were
more used to handling weapons. In any case, they made
very good soldiers. On the Southern side, the same was
true—even more so. A larger percentage of the men
came from rural areas because there were fewer cities in
the South. A number of them didn't even bother with
shoes, but they were very, very bad boys to get into a
fight with.

The war was greeted in its first few weeks almost as a
festival. Everybody seemed relieved. People went out
and celebrated, both in the North and in the South.
There were parades, bands playing, flags flying; people
seemed almost happy. Large numbers of troops were
enlisted; as a matter of fact, again in both the North and
South, more men offered themselves than could be handled. Neither the Union nor the Confederate governments had the weapons, uniforms, or anything else to
equip all of the men who tried to enlist.

Both armies contained a number of very ardent teen-
agers who had lied about their age in order to get into
the army in the first place. Legal age, of course, was
eighteen. It turned out that, in the North at least, a very
common little gag had been developed. A boy who was
under eighteen and wanted to enlist, would take a piece
of paper and scribble the figure eighteen on it. Then he
would take off his shoe, placing the piece of paper into
the sole of his shoe, put it back on and tie it up. He
would go to the recruiting station and, since he would
obviously be looking rather young, sooner or later the
recruiting officer would look at him and say "How old
are you, son?" Then, the boy, in perfect honesty, could
say "I am over eighteen."

The point about that is not so much that young men were lying about their age in order to get into the army, but they would go to the trouble of working out a gag like that. A man simply wouldn't dream of taking an oath that he was eighteen when he wasn't. Lying to the government was a little beyond him, but he would work out a thing like this and could say honestly, "I'm over eighteen" and that made it quite all right.

A set of statistics was compiled about the average Northern soldier that are rather interesting. They apply pretty much to the South as well. An average soldier was 5 feet, 8¼ inches tall; he weighed just over 143 pounds. Forty-eight percent were farmers; 24 percent were mechanics; 15 percent were laborers; 5 percent were businessmen, and 3 percent were professional men. That was really a kind of cross-section of the population of the United States at that time. About one-half farmers, about 40 percent working men, and 10 percent businessmen or professionals.

When a man joined the Union army he was given shoes that must have been a little bit of a trial to wear. In a great many cases, army contractors simply made the right and left shoe identical. They were squared off at the toe and it didn't matter which one you put on which foot; they were supposed to work either way. They must have been very uncomfortable, and I imagine they account for a great many of the cases of footsore soldiers who fell out on the march and stumbled into camp long after everybody else had gone to bed.

The Civil War soldier, on the Northern side, at least, got a great deal to eat; the trouble was that most of it was not very good. The Union army enlisted no cooks or bakers during the entire war. Originally, each man was supposed to cook for himself. It happened, of course, practically immediately, that company kitchens were established. Men were detailed from the ranks to act as cooks; some of them cooked fairly well and some of them, of course, cooked abominably. But whatever they cooked, the boys ate.

The basic ration for the Civil War soldier, particularly on the march where it was not possible to carry along vegetables, was salt pork or bacon and hardtack. The hardtack was a big soda cracker, quite thick and, as the name implies, very tough—made tough so that it wouldn't fall into pieces while it was joggling about in a man's haversack. When the hardtack was fresh, it was apparently quite good to eat. The trouble is that it was very rarely fresh. Boxes of hardtack would sit on railroad platforms or sidetracked in front of warehouses for weeks and months at a time and, by the time the soldier got them, they were often infested and not very good.

Every soldier carried some sort of a tin can in which he could boil coffee. Coffee was issued in the whole bean, for when the government issued ground coffee, they could never quite trust the contractors not to adulterate it. When the soldier made coffee he would put a handful of beans in a bucket and grind them with the butt of his musket. In the morning, in camp, you could tell when the boys were getting up by the rhythmic clinking, grinding noise that came up from in front of every tent.

The soldier also had sugar to go with his coffee and he would boil his coffee in his little tin can and then dump in some sugar. He would usually have a skillet in which to fry his bacon. Sometimes he would crumble up hard-tack and drop the crumbs in the sizzling bacon fat and make a rather indescribable mess—I guess a healthy young man who got a good deal of exercise could digest it without too much difficulty.

In the Civil War, which lasted four years, about 600,000 young Americans, North and South together, lost their lives. That is not the total casualty list; it is the number that actually went under the sod. The wounded, the missing, the prisoners, were in another list. Six hundred thousand is the number of lives that were actually lost.

If you want to understand what a terrible drain that was on the country, reflect that the total population in the United States in the 1860s was about an eighth or a ninth of what it is today. The number of men killed in that war, if you interpret it in today's terms, would come to something between four and four and one-half million. In other words, a perfectly frightful toll of American lives was taken.

There are a good many reasons why the toll was so high. More than *one half* of the men who died were not killed in action; they simply died of camp diseases: typhoid fever, pneumonia, dysentery, and childhood diseases like measles and chicken pox.

To begin with, medical science then was woefully inadequate. Doctors simply did not know what caused such devastating camp diseases as typhoid fever, which accounted for about one fourth of all deaths in army hospitals. Malaria, a plague of the Virginia swamp country, was attributed to "miasmic vapors" arising from stagnant waters and not to the pestiferous mosquitoes bred therein. (The vapors were also largely blamed for typhoid and dysentery.) Nothing was known about how and why wounds became infected, and so nothing much was done to prevent infection; surgeons talked soberly about "laudable pus" which was expected to appear a few days after an operation or a gunshot wound, its laudable character arising because it showed that the body was discharging poisons.

The number of men who simply got sick and died, or who got a minor scratch or cut and then could do nothing to check the infection, was appalling. Just to be in the army in the 1860s was much more dangerous than anything we know about today, even though many a man in the army never got into action. It was a very common thing—in fact, almost the rule—for a Civil War regiment on either side to lose about half of its strength either in men who became sick and died or men who became so ill they had to get medical discharges before the regiment ever saw action. Whereas a Civil War regiment, on paper, contained about one thousand men, in actual fact, a regiment that went into battle with as many as five hundred men was quite fortunate.

* * *

Not long after the war began, whenever a Northern and Southern army were camped fairly close to each other, the men on the picket lines would get acquainted with one another and would call little informal truces. The Northern soldiers would bring in coffee to trade. Along the Rappahannock River, they made quite a thing of constructing little toy boats out of planks. A boat would be maybe two feet long, with a mast and a sail. Loaded with coffee, it would be sent out into the stream, pointed south, and when it would get across the river, the Confederate soldiers would unload the coffee, stock it with tobacco, and send it back.

This led to some rather odd happenings, since men who are stopping to trade with each other are apt to get a little friendly along the way. There was one rather famous occasion, again along the Rappahannock River, when in a building not far behind the Confederate lines back of the outposts, there was going to be a dance one evening, and the Confederate pickets invited their Yankee friends to come over and go to the dance.

Half a dozen Yankee soldiers, leaving their guns behind them, crossed the river in the darkness, went to the dance and had a very good time—until a Confederate officer appeared just when festivities were at their height. He was, of course, horrified, and ordered the Yankee soldiers arrested and thrown into prison, at which point the Confederates begged him not to do this. They said they had given the Yankees their word that everything would be all right if they came to the dance, and asked that the officer let them go.

Well, the officer saw some point to that appeal. He couldn't violate or cause his men to violate their honor, so after giving all hands a don't-let-it-happen-again lecture he released the Yankee prisoners and they went home, with a good dance under their belts.

Along the Rapidan River during the winter of 1863 and 1864, the armies for a number of miles had outposts that were drawn up very close to each other. In fact, in

one or two places, they actually overlapped. The
Yankees had a way of advancing their picket lines in the
night and pulling them back in the daytime. The Confederates did it just the other way around; their picket
lines were a little farther forward by day than by night.
Pretty soon it turned out that there was a picket post,
with a log cabin and a fireplace, that was used at night
by the Yankees and in the daytime by the Confederates.
The boys worked out a deal: Each party would leave a
stack of firewood on hand and be sure to get out before
the other one got there. They kept on that way quite
pleasantly for some months.

At the great Battle of Fredericksburg, down at the far
end of the line where the fighting was not very heavy,
there was a woodland stretch held by the Confederates
on one side and the Yankees on the other. The pickets,
again, were quite close together, and the skirmish lines
not much farther apart. The men got to cat-calling and
jeering at each other and making insulting remarks.
This went on for quite a while in much the same way
that a couple of high school football cheering sections
might yell back and forth at each other. Finally, a
couple of soldiers, a Confederate and a Yankee, got
really angry. They got so angry that they had to have a
fight. So all along the line in this particular section of
the woodland, the soldiers called an informal truce, and
the riled-up Yankee and Southerner got out and had a
very fine, soul-satisfying fist fight. I don't know who
came out on top, but at last the fight ended, as all such
fights do, and the men went to a nearby stream and
washed the blood off their faces and shook hands. Then
both sides went back, picked up their weapons, and
started shooting at each other again.

It was that kind of war. Rather informal, and fought
between men who, when left alone, got along together
beautifully. You've often heard it spoken of as the War
Between Brothers. Actually, it really was that.

The siege of Vicksburg was another case where the
picket lines were so close together that on one occasion
the Southerners and the Northerners had a little meeting

and came to an agreement as to just where the picket lines ought to go, so they wouldn't trespass on each other's territory.

During this siege, one of the Confederates out on the picket line asked if there were any Missouri regiments in the army immediately opposing his section. He was a Missourian himself and was looking for his brother. The Yankees made inquiry and pretty soon they came forward with the Confederate soldier's brother—both boys from Missouri, one of them in Confederate gray and the other in Federal blue. The Confederate had a roll of bills in his hand and gave them to his brother to send to their mother, who was peaceably at home in Missouri. He couldn't get things out from Vicksburg through the Union lines, Vicksburg being completely surrounded, so he asked his brother to send them to her, and the brother did. There was no shooting while these arrangements were made, then the brothers shook hands, retired to their individual lines, and the shooting started up again.

During the fighting at Crampton's Gap in Maryland in the fall of 1862, the Confederates were slowly withdrawing. They were fighting a rearguard action rather than a regular battle. One Yankee soldier got a little too far forward, slipped, and accidentally slid down the side of the steep hill on which he had been posted, winding up at the bottom of the hill in a thicket. There he confronted a Confederate soldier who wasn't ready to retreat yet. The two men grabbed their guns. But eventually they figured there was no point in shooting each other here, off in a quiet corner where there wasn't much going on, so they laid down their weapons and made an agreement. They would stay where they were with no shooting. At the end of the day if the Confederates had advanced, the Yankee would be the Confederate soldier's prisoner. If the Yankees had advanced, then the Confederate would be the Yankee's prisoner. Meanwhile, there wasn't any sense in getting shot. The Confederates eventually withdrew, and the Yankee soldier found he had taken a prisoner.

One of the most touching stories I know involving this acquaintanceship—friendship, really—between the rival soldiers took place at Fredericksburg, Virginia, along the Rappahannock, a couple of months after the big battle there. The Rappahannock River is not very wide, and the men on the northern bank could easily talk with the men on the southern bank if they raised their voices a little. One winter afternoon when nothing much was going on, a number of the Federal army bands were massed on the hillside overlooking the river valley to give a little informal concert. They played all of the Northern patriotic songs, and the Northern soldiers crowded around to listen. On the opposite shore, the Confederate soldiers gathered to enjoy the concert.

After a while, the band had pretty well run through its repertoire and there was a pause, whereupon some of the Confederates shouted, "Now play some of ours." So, the band began to play Southern tunes. They played "Dixie" and "Bonnie Blue Flag" and "Yellow Rose of Texas" and I don't know what all. They played Southern tunes while the Southern and Northern armies sat in the quiet and listened.

It was getting on toward dusk by this time, so the band, to signal the end of the concert, went into "Home, Sweet Home." Both armies together tried to sing it, and it was rather a sentimental occasion. After all, these boys were a long way from home. They knew perfectly well that a great many of them were never going to see home again; as soon as the warm weather came, they would be fighting each other. The song got to be a little too much for them and pretty soon they got choked up and couldn't sing, and the band finished the music all by itself.

A couple of months later, the troops faced each other in the terrible Battle of Chancellorsville.

Army of Innocents

Training camp, in the days of Julius Caesar and at the present moment, is a place where raw recruits are worked over until they are fit to go out and be killed with proper military formality. At certain times and places it is done much better than at others, but the story is more or less the same everywhere. You learn to do things by the numbers, you keep your mouth shut because you get into trouble if you don't, and before the business is over, you are thoroughly indoctrinated in the army's way of doing things. It is extremely important that you get thus indoctrinated because if you don't, you will probably behave disgracefully when it is time to go out and get killed. And as a matter of fact, you are much more likely to survive that dreadful day if you have had the army way drilled into you. There is no more vulnerable creature on earth than the untaught innocent on a battlefield.

To remove vulnerability and innocence, accordingly, was one of the chief functions of the training camp. Up

to a certain point, the Civil War camp did this very well.
The removal of innocence was easy—no army has ever
had any trouble with that—but the removal of
vulnerability was something else again. It involved the
creation of a certain battlefield sophistication among
young men whose wildest dreams never told them what
a battlefield was really like, and unfortunately very few
of the officers at these camps knew any more than the
trainees. This was because of a fundamental defect in
the way the volunteer armies of the 1860s were
organized. The government had devised an excellent
system for getting recruits, but its very excellence made
it very difficult for the training camp to do its job.

The army was raised by the states. The basic unit was
the regiment which, on paper at any rate, consisted of
about a thousand men of all ranks. Only after a
regiment was complete were the men sworn into Federal
service. Once this happened, they were part of the
national army; but until it happened, they belonged to
the states.

This meant that the state governor was all-important
at the start. It was he who named the officers and saw to
it that the men were enlisted, and while he needed (and
almost invariably got) the full cooperation of the state
legislature, and needed also things like uniforms and
weapons which the Federal Government would provide,
it was largely up to him to make certain that his state
met its quota when enlistments were called for. To do
this, he naturally called on various and sundry leading
citizens for help—men of stature and influence in village
and city, in county and Congressional district, and in
the state as a whole. To bind these men to the cause, the
governor would give them tentative commissions in the
new regiment, the commissions to become permanent as
soon as the regiment was raised and sworn in.

This brought in recruits with a rush, which went all
the faster because (in the war's first year, at least) so
many thousands of young men were determined to enlist
as quickly as possible. It is easy to see how it worked. In
a typical northern county, for instance, there might be,

in the county seat or elsewhere, a man of some prominence—a lawyer, say, or a businessman, a miller, or a schoolteacher—who was tolerably well-known in his neighborhood and apparently gifted with some capacity for leadership. This man would be given a captaincy, and it was up to him to raise a full company of one hundred men. He began usually by finding a couple of local activists to serve as lieutenants, got the governor to commission them, and with them set out to get recruits. The recruits, of course, all came from the same neighborhood, often enough from the same township. Mostly, they knew each other and knew the captain and lieutenants, before they ever signed up. This process was repeated ten times, and presently there were ten companies off in boot camp, complete with colonel, field officers, company and platoon commanders, and all the rest; complete also with uniforms and with a sense that they were off on a great adventure. Presently, the whole outfit was mustered into Federal service, and the training could begin.

The flaws in the officer-selection system came to light almost at once. In most cases, the officers knew no more about fighting than the enlisted men. They had everything to learn—even the routine movements of ordinary infantry drill—and while they learned they had to teach the men under them. The colonel was supposed to conduct officer-training classes at night so that the officers, next morning, could go out and instruct the soldiers. Inasmuch as the colonel usually knew no more about it than the officers he called into class, the business sometimes took some odd turns. Most officers were conscientious, however, and more than one colonel stayed up until after midnight cramming with the books that enlarged upon the way regimental and company officers should behave. By and large, it worked out better than one would expect.

There were helpful factors here and there. Some officers had had a good deal of militia experience, which was not exactly soldiering the way the Regulars practiced it, but did at least provide a foundation. Here and there, a veteran of the war with Mexico showed up; and now and then—rarely, at first, but in increasing numbers as the war went on—genuine West Pointers took volunteer army colonelcies and undertook to get green officers and enlistees trained on a proper basis.

The untamed recruits did not always like the West Pointers who came in to take charge of them. A home-county colonel or major could usually be talked to, man to man. He was not likely to be too rigid with soldiers whose families knew his family back home and who, in many cases, had been on a first-name basis with him and would be so again when the war ended. The West Pointer was more remote, and any hometown influence your father or Uncle Pete might have meant nothing to him. Eventually, however, the boys came to see that there were compensations.

An officer from the Regular Army might have his prickly side, but he had been thoroughly indoctrinated with the idea that a good officer looks after his men. A West Point colonel would frequently visit the cook shack, for instance, examining and sampling the food the enlisted men were getting, and giving the cooks or the commissary officers a sturdy blowing-up if it was not up to standard. He would see to it that a man whose shoes were worn out got a new pair, and he knew little tricks like having all hands dig shallow trenches around their tents so that a rainstorm falling on a side hill camp would not flood everybody out. The chronic malingerers who developed mysterious ailments just in time to miss a day's fatigue or drill on a hot August morning usually got short shrift from him, but a man who was genuinely ailing could find himself sent off to the doctor before he himself realized that he ought to be put to bed for a few days. (The care he got in a typical training camp hospital might be highly defective, but it was all that was available, and a Regular officer would at least see to it that the men who needed it most got it.)

The real mischief that was done by the system used to select officers for the volunteers came later on, after the regiment had left the training camp and gone on duty

with one of the invading armies. Discipline was in-
curably loose. It was bound to be for it was widely held
that free-born Americans should not be governed by the
strict controls used by the Regulars. American life being
what it is, a high proportion of the volunteer officers
planned to run for office once they got back home, and
the men they now commanded would then be men they
had to canvass for votes. To be unduly strict now might
easily be to estrange a future voter, and no politician in
his senses wanted to do that. Even if no politicking was
involved, the soldier was all too likely to see his captain
or lieutenant not as the embodiment of the stern majesty
of inflexible military law, but as Good Old Tom who
would take a reasonable view of things simply because
he was a Good Guy and an Old Friend.

This actually proved less a problem in battle than it
was between battles. In battle, these hometown officers,
very anxious to do their full duty under fire, took on a
stiffness they did not ordinarily exhibit, and much the
same thing was true of the enlisted men. They felt their
responsibility and they did their best to live up to it, and
although there were failures here and there, the Civil
War records of the volunteer armies on both sides is an
amazing display of enduring heroism. The hitch, of
course, lay in the fact that these brave soldiers were
quite likely to decide for themselves when they had done
enough. The taut, impersonal discipline that could hold
them in place after they made that decision did not exist.
Even the good regiments suffered a steady leakage of
men to the rear during a hot action. The apparent battlefield losses were always greater than the real losses. In
a day or so the stragglers would drift back into camp;
for the most part they were men who had done their full
duty up to a point, but it was the individual private and
not a higher authority who decided when that point had
been reached.

It was on the march, however, that this lack of tight
discipline showed up most clearly. The ordinary Civil
War regiment, North as well as South, straggled abominably when it moved from here to there. At the end of a

long day's march, less than half of the present-for-duty regimental strength might be on hand to make camp; the absentees would come ambling in at all hours, disturbing the rest of the men who had gone to sleep and in general making a farce out of the appointed routine. Some of these were men who honestly could not see why any harm was done by straggling, as long as they reached the regiment that night. The stragglers inevitably included, however, all of the sad sacks and hooligans on the roster. Roving about the countryside all along the army's line of march, they foraged and looted with a free hand. They bore down most heavily in the enemy's country, telling themselves that it was time the enemy civilians felt the weight of the war. But they were not gentle with their own civilians either, and a farmer whose chickens and swine survived the marchpast of an army was extremely lucky. The excesses committed by Federal troops on Sherman's famous march across Georgia came only in part from the commanding general's demand that the invaded country support his column. Most of it derived from the fact that the stragglers were totally out from under control on this march. Some of them, indeed, found this prolonged Halloween existence so much fun that they never did get back into ranks.

It was not just on Sherman's march that straggling proved so costly—after all, between Atlanta and the sea Sherman's men did very little fighting, and if the ranks were not full when the day began, not much was lost. But armies that did have to fight and needed full ranks up front suffered abominably. There was a steady fading-away process that set in when the first flutter of far-off gun fire set the air quivering over the horizon, and as this noise deepened and became recognizable as the sound of battle, the fading-away intensified. When a brigade left the road, crossed half a mile of farmland, and then shook itself out into line of battle amid such thickets, ditches, swamps, and clumps of underbrush as might exist, it rarely brought into line as many men as it took off the road. When this line came under fire the

leakage increased. If a wounded man had to go to the
rear, there would be several comrades to help him, and
these usually had trouble finding their way back to the
firing line. The immediate rear of the scene of action
was usually cluttered with uninjured men who had "got
lost" and whose attempts to find their proper places had
somehow led them farther and farther to the rear. Eventually, the authorities posted cavalry pickets behind the
front, and when they saw a displaced infantryman, their
curt order (delivered over drawn sabers) was: "Show
blood!" If he could not do this, the foot soldier was
driven back into line. The imperfect grip so many company officers had on their men was most expensive
when the showdown of actual combat put discipline to
the test.

One extremely surprising shortcoming in many camps
of instruction appears when the battle records of individual regiments are examined. In a great many cases,
nobody taught the raw recruit how to load and fire his
rifle. That such a failure should exist seems incredible,
but the records speak for themselves. At the battle of
Shiloh there is an account of one green regiment under
fire which suddenly realized that no one had ever shown
it how to use its weapons. From a more-experienced
regiment nearby, veterans came over and passed along
the greenhorns' battle line, giving quick instruction in
the basic task of the soldier. It is written that the recruits
caught on quickly enough—being under a brisk Confederate fire must have been a powerful stimulus to the
learning process—and the regiment stayed and fought,
although it is permissible to doubt that the shots it fired
hit anyone except by accident.

Much more graphic is an illustration from the awesome Battle of Gettysburg, where all of the troops involved were supposed to be veterans. After the battle,
Meade's ordnance officers combed the littered field,
collecting 37,000 rifles that had been abandoned. They
found that more than a third of these were loaded with
more than one cartridge—some of them with as many as
half a dozen. The men who owned those rifles had had

some training but not enough. They knew how to tear cartridge, pour powder down the barrel and then ram a bullet down on top of it. But no one had ever shown them that it was necessary then to put a percussion cap under the hammer of the weapon, and without the cap in place, a soldier might pull trigger all day without firing the piece. (In the clamorous confusion of battle the untrained soldier might not even realize that his rifle had not gone off. If he had fired his piece before, he would, of course, notice that his uncapped weapon failed to recoil against his shoulder, but if he had had no experience on the rifle range, this negative bit of evidence would mean nothing. It goes without saying, of course, that a soldier who did put a cap on one of those rifles with six loads in the barrel, and then pulled the trigger, would get his face blown into the next county.) After he digested this news, General Meade ordered regimental commanders to make certain that every man in the ranks got in a little firing practice.

In the long run, the Civil War training camp aimed to give the recruit a basic understanding of military life, with actual combat training coming in on-the-job contact with the enemy. This was unquestionably learning a trade the hard way; what kept it from being totally disastrous was the fact that when imperfectly trained Union troops went into battle they fought against Confederates whose training had been no better than their own. When they set out to kill each other, these armies taught each other.

A Rich Man's War
—a Poor Man's Fight

What we have been talking about so far are the early regiments—the volunteer regiments, which were made up largely of men who were in the army simply because they wanted to be in it.

After the first year or two the crop of volunteers dwindled almost to the vanishing point. The Federal Government, like the Confederate government, was obliged to resort to conscription. The only trouble was that the Congress in Washington adopted probably the worst conscription law anybody ever imagined. It had two very bad features; first, a man whose number was drawn for drafting could pay a $300 commutation fee and get excused from service. His number might be drawn again later, but, unless and until it was, his payment of a $300 fee excused him. Consequently the well-to-do man could not be forced into the army and the poor man could. Bear in mind that in 1862, $300 was a very fair year's income for an unskilled laborer. Even a skilled mechanic would not make twice that much money in a year, and in the ordinary course of things, never actually saw as much as $300 in cash.

An even worse feature of the draft act was the fact that it permitted a man who had been drafted to hire a substitute. If he could find some man who was willing to fight if paid, he would pay him whatever the market rate called for and the man would go and fill the draftee's place. If he got killed, that was too bad; but the draftee himself was off the hook. The Civil War had quickly become what the common soldiers on both sides called it—a Rich Man's War, and a Poor Man's Fight.

Technically, the draft did not put a great many men into uniform. That is, the number of drafted men who became soldiers was comparatively small. What the draft did do and what made it very important to the Government, was to stimulate recruiting drives by states, cities, and other government organizations. The draft, which was very unpopular, would not be applied in any locality that had met its quota of recruits. The country was divided up into Congressional Districts; its need for men was apportioned to those districts, and each district was supposed to provide a specific number of men. If that proper number of men had volunteered in a given district, the draft would not apply there. So, it was in the interest of government authorities in the counties and cities to recruit men as vigorously as they could, simply to keep the draft from affecting the people in that area. In that way, the draft was extremely effective. It stirred recruiting drives all over the country and resulted in a great many men going into the army who probably would not have enlisted if they were left to their own devices.

The draft also caused a great many substitutes to go to war; at least 75,000 men were hired by drafted civilians. In addition, about 42,000 men were paid to go into the army as substitutes by men who were enrolled in the draft and were simply trying to do their best to support the war effort. Oddly enough, one of the men who sent a substitute in his place was Abraham Lincoln himself. He, of course, was not subject to the draft, but he

did hire a substitute and the man served a full term in
the army and apparently acquitted himself very well.

So, between the added number of volunteers and the
substitutes who were paid directly by draftees or other
stay-at-homes, the Conscription Act did bring a large
number of men into the army.

With all of the great defects in the Civil War Draft
Law, it was inevitable that the enforcement of the law
would be attended by grave difficulties. These were
much more serious than anything we have seen in this
country since then. In New York City, for instance, in
the summer of 1863, very shortly after the time of the
Battle of Gettysburg, one of the worst riots that ever afflicted any American city broke out because of the
draft. The riot started at a Provost Marshal's office in
mid-Manhattan, where draft numbers were being
drawn. People gathered outside, objecting to the whole
process, and soon started throwing bricks through the
windows. Emotions exploded, and the mob destroyed
the office, beat up the people who were in it, and went
rampaging through town. Because of the violence, the
Draft Act had to be suspended in New York City and
the militia had to be called out. But the militia was
unable to cope with the situation and the mob got completely out of control. It set fires and lynched as many
black people as it could lay its hands on. It burned down
a black orphanage and did its best to destroy the people
who came out of the burning building. All in all, in the
course of a week about a thousand were killed or
wounded. In the end, regiments had to be brought in
from the Army of the Potomac, fresh from the battlefield at Gettysburg, to restore order.

Whereas the draft riots in New York City were by far
the worst of any during the Civil War, they were by no
means the only ones. A very serious situation developed
in the anthracite coal-mining regions of Pennsylvania,
where the coal miners, who tended to be a downtrodden
class of laborers at that period of the country's development, were trying to form a union and get some sort of
decent pay and working conditions in the mines. While

they were doing this, the draft came along, and it did
seem to happen that very often the men who had been
the most active in promoting unionization were the first
ones to be picked up by the Provost Marshal and taken
off to the army. The coal miners rioted up and down the
countryside, tearing down draft offices and in general
defying the authorities. Again, troops had to be sent in
to tone things down and restore order.

As a matter of fact, order was restored finally by dint
of some fast footwork on the part of President Lincoln
who, I think, had a certain amount of sympathy for
what the coal miners were up against. Lincoln worked
out, or at least consented to, a very neat little arrangement that rested on the Congressional District alloca-
tion. There was an obscure provision in the Draft Act
stating that a man should be credited to the Congressional District from which he came, rather than the one
in which he actually enlisted. That is, if a man living in
Meadeville, Pennsylvania, happened to be in Philadelphia and enlisted there, his enlistment should be
credited to the district back home in Meadeville. It
rarely happened, but that was the theory.

Some people got to work and examined the returns in
Eastern Pennsylvania and discovered, or claimed they
discovered, that hundreds of men who had been enlisted
in Philadelphia actually came from the anthracite
regions and that these regions had, consequently, met
their quotas. As a result, the draft was finally suspended
in the anthracite areas, and things went on very
smoothly.

There were other cases where troops had to be called
in. There was actually a small military engagement in
north-central Ohio where the farmers dug in around
some isolated woodland and announced their defiance
of the Government. Troops were sent up from Colum-
bus, and a few shots were fired, without doing a great
deal of harm to anybody, before this uprising was put
down.

The draft was obviously extremely unpopular. No
Congressman and no member of the State Legislature

wanted to see his people drafted, so the state and local
governments came to the rescue.

A city or town would offer a bounty to any man who
enlisted voluntarily; the County Board of Com-
missioners would add its own fee to that; the State
Legislature might add some more, and leading citizens
might raise a fund. Toward the final year and a half of
the war, the bounties got so high that a man could get
anywhere from five hundred to a thousand dollars simply for enlisting. Substitute brokers began to appear in
the cities; that is, men who would find volunteers for a
man who didn't want to serve the time himself. They
would get paid out of the bounty which the enlistee
would get, and they rode herd on him to see that they
got it.

It also led to the development, all across the North, of
a class of men known as bounty jumpers. A man would
come in and enlist, draw his bounty, desert again, enlist
in still a third place, and keep this up as long as he could
get away with it. There are reports of men who had
enlisted as many as six or eight times. These men, of
course, were of no earthly use as soldiers. It was hard
enough to get them to the front at all; they had to be
kept constantly under guard. There are a number of accounts of convoys accompanied by armed guards
coming down from the North to the camps in Virginia.
As deserters or bounty jumpers tried to jump off the
train, they came under fire—and some were killed.
Many, of course, got away.

If they actually had to join the army in camp, they
would desert the first time they got into battle. Often
they would allow themselves to be captured, for the
Confederacy let it be known that they needed workers in
war plants in the South, that wages were high, that any
prisoner of war who wanted to go to work in a factory
in Richmond, Atlanta, or where ever, would be
welcomed and well paid. They got quite a lot of men
that way. The men, of course, were not worth any more
as workers than they were as soldiers, and, in 1864 the
Confederacy withdrew this offer.

General Grant remarked at the end of the war that not one soldier in eight who was brought in by the high-bounty system ever did any useful service at the front. The men in the ranks, themselves, abominated these high-bounty troops; they ostracized them. They did their best to shove them up into the front lines where they would at least get shot at before they could surrender. Whenever they could, they made life uncomfortable for them, and there are lots of ways you can do that in the army.

Amid all of this, the men who were actually drafted, the men who couldn't hire a substitute and couldn't pay the commutation fee, usually turned out to be fairly good soldiers. Even to the end, the Union army depended primarily on the volunteers. In the winter of 1863-64, especially along in January and February of 1864, the army had to do an enormous job of recruiting because the term of service for most of the soldiers in those days was three years. Those men who had enlisted at the start of the war, the enthusiastic, ardent men, the men who made by far the best soldiers, were running out of time; their enlistments were about to expire. There was no way on earth the government could compel them to stay in the army if they didn't want to. The government had already given these soldiers an object lesson about the folly of volunteering through its abominable conscription act. Then, it suddenly had to go to these men, hat in hand, and ask them to reenlist.

It's amazing, but many of them did stay on. These were men who had been through the mill. They had been through the terrible battles—Shiloh, Chancellorsville, Gettysburg, and Chickamauga. They had survived them, knew what it was like, and knew that even worse fights were coming. They had done their duty and were entitled to go home. In spite of all this, many of them voluntarily reenlisted. The percentage was a good deal higher in the Western armies than it was in the Army of the Potomac, but even in the Army of the Potomac, close to 30,000 volunteers reenlisted that winter of 1863-64; a larger number did so in the West.

If a regiment could show a certain percentage of its number reenlisting, it was entitled thereafter to call itself a Veteran Volunteer Regiment, and that was a title the men prized very, very highly, particularly after the war. If they had belonged to a Veteran Volunteer Regiment, they were sure to mention the fact.

In one way or another, the Union army managed to keep itself at adequate strength and carry on with the war. It should be noted that the Confederate government was a great deal wiser. It came to a draft act earlier and, after a very brief experience with such loopholes as substitutes, it tightened its rules and made the draft a fair, workable act. It did not have nearly the trouble the Northern government had; its major problem was that it didn't have as many men from which to draw. What helped to cripple the Confederacy as much as anything, probably, was the fact that so many of its factories and its railroad system—actually all of its transportation systems—were fatally handicapped because the army had drained off the manpower. It didn't have enough men to both run the war plants and keep the army at proper strength. It could do one or the other, but it couldn't do both. Because the war plants couldn't operate at full strength, because the railroads were so run down that the supply services kept collapsing, the strain on the soldiers was great. They had to get along with inadequate food and clothing; they were poorly shod, as often as not, and they had no tents. Toward the final year of the war, when the picture was getting even darker and the Northern armies were advancing deeper and deeper into the South, the Confederate armies were profoundly affected by a very high rate of desertion.

By the end of 1864, of the men on the Southern army rolls, there were probably as many at home as with the colors. The mainspring had broken; the men who elected to go home and look after their families can't be blamed. Their government was unable to take care of their families for them, and they had stood all that any soldiers could properly be asked to stand.

So, in the final months of the war, the Confederate

armies ran down and, as they did so, the Union armies began to get a new source of recruits. A great many of the veterans whose time had expired in the spring of 1864 and who went back home to enjoy life as civilians, began, by the end of the year, to drift back into the army. Some of the regiments that were formed at the end of 1864 and the beginning of 1865 were first-rate regiments because they were full of veteran soldiers— not bounty jumpers, not hired substitutes, but men who knew their way around in the army and who had come back because they apparently wanted to be in at the finish. They could see the war being won, and they wanted to be there when it was won.

Lost from the Army

Deserters, of course, all through the Civil War, were extremely numerous. There was probably a much higher rate of desertion in the Civil War than in any other war we have ever had. (I am speaking now of the situation in the North. Although, in the end, the number of desertions in the South was extremely high, throughout most of the war the desertion problem was not quite the same in the South as it was in the North.) In the North, during the year 1864, desertions averaged 7,300 every month. A great many of these people actually never put on a uniform at all. They simply refused to respond when drafted and quietly disappeared. Although they actually never saw the army, they were listed as deserters.

A great many more went "over the hill," as the expression goes. There were a good many ways to do this. The sheer inefficiency of the system the Government had set up to check desertions was their greatest reliance. They took advantage of all kinds of opportunities that are not open to soldiers today.

For example, fairly early in the war, the Government

opened a set of home-state hospitals for sick or
wounded soldiers on the theory that a man who required
hospitalization would recover best if he could be
transferred back to a hospital in his own state. This
was a very good thing for the soldiers, and it did help
recovery and was a humanitarian step on the part of the
Government. The trouble was that it opened the door
wide for the deserter. A man who was transferred from
a hospital in, say, northern Virginia to a hospital
back in Indiana went completely out from under the
control of the army. He was put under the control of
the local hospital authorities, who were answerable
to nobody but the Surgeon General of the United States
Army. His own Company Commander, his Regimental
Commander, his Army Commander, couldn't touch
him. The only people who had any control over him
were the authorities of the local hospital.

Since these hospitals were staffed on a patronage
basis by men appointed by the governor, they had very
strong political tie-ins with the reigning state government and, as a result, were open to all kinds of political
pressure. Therefore, they were in no hurry to send men
back to the army after the men had recovered. On the
contrary, a man who had any political pull at all could
get his stay prolonged indefinitely. If he had any little
skills which could be useful around the hospital—if he
could build chicken coops or wash windows or do
anything of that kind—he would be detailed to work
there as a convalescent patient and might possibly be
kept there for the rest of the war.

Also, it was very easy for him to get a furlough from
the state hospital to go back to his own home and see his
folks. Again, the theory was that this would hasten his
recovery. When he got the furlough, however, there was
nobody with any particular interest in seeing that he
came back. The people at the hospital didn't especially
care; he was way out of the reach of his own Company
and Regimental Commander, and he could always get a
certificate from his local doctor saying that his health
just was not very good and would be better if he were
allowed to stay home a little longer. If he wanted to, he

could simply drift away and forget about coming back altogether.

One of the more foolish things that the Federal Government did when the war started was to change the rewards which had always been offered to civilian peace officers for the arrest of army deserters. Until 1861 a policeman or deputy sheriff or constable who arrested a deserter and held him for the army authorities got a reward of $30, which was not bad money in those days. For some quite incomprehensible reason, after the war started this $30 was reduced to $5.00. In addition, the officer who claimed the reward had to prepare and submit a long set of documents showing what his expenses were, how he had incurred them, and why it was necessary to incur them at all. Since that was the era of red tape at its greatest in Government financial offices, any Government paymaster could keep a policeman at bay for a year with all of these documents. As a result, no cop in his senses would bother to arrest a deserter unless the deserter went out of his way to make himself obnoxious. It was just more trouble than it was worth. Consequently, a deserter, if he kept moderately quiet, was in little danger of being picked up and sent back.

Thinking about the men who ran away leads one to a consideration of the men who were actually taken prisoner; not the men who dropped their weapons and let themselves be captured in order to get out of fighting, but the honest, well-intentioned soldier who was captured in the heat of battle. If you captured a substantial number of your enemy's troops, it was not always necessary to take them back to a prison camp and assume the burden of controlling and feeding them. You could release them on parole; that is, on their word, signed by the individual soldiers and their officers, that they would not take up arms again unless they had been formally exchanged by action of their own government and the government with which it was making war.

The point was that each side had a number of prisoners on its hands. It was to everybody's advantage

to release them on parole. As long as the two governments could trust one another and not cheat unduly on
this business, the parole was an advantageous system all
around.

During the Civil War, that point of mutual trust was
still good. So the North maintained parole camps for its
own men who had been captured in the South and
released; the South maintained parole camps for Confederate soldiers who had been captured by the
Northerners and released.

Now and then, through cumbersome but effective
processes of negotiation, the two governments would
work out exchanges. The parole prisoners would be
notified that their paroles were lifted and they were
to go back to the army. This did not always work very
well because men on parole tended to feel that they
were out of the war, and because parole camps were
usually not very well disciplined. Often the men simply
drifted away from them, and so it wasn't always easy
for a general whose soldiers were released from parole
to get them all back into service. Grant himself argued,
when he granted parole to Pemberton's soldiers at
Vicksburg, that no matter what happened in the way of
exchange, the bulk of these men would never return to
the Confederate service.

When Grant became General-in-Chief in March of
1864, he realized that a great many more Confederate
soldiers had been captured than Northern soldiers, and
the Confederacy was more hard pressed for manpower.
He therefore discontinued the parole system and refused
to make any more exchanges, believing that they ben-
efited the Confederacy more than they did the North.
As a result, both sides were obliged to develop large
prison camps. Andersonville Prison in Georgia came
into existence because of this. In the North there were
equally large and almost equally uncomfortable prison
camps for Confederate soldiers.

I don't think any institution in the Civil War received
quite such a bad press as the prison camp. The most
notorious was, of course, the one at Andersonville,

where for a long time, thirty thousand men were herded
together without any shelter except what they themselves could put together, and where the death rate was
fantastically high—probably between ten and fifteen
thousand Union soldiers lost their lives there. After the
war, the one man who was tried and executed as a war
criminal was Henry C. Wirz, the Confederate officer
who was in charge of Andersonville.

The conditions at Andersonville were fully as bad as
all of the stories say they were. But Andersonville was
not very much worse than other camps. It was very little
worse, for instance, than some of the camps the North
maintained for Confederate prisoners. One that was
particularly bad was the one at Elmira, New York,
where, to this day, there are a large number of Confederate graves. The complaints about the situation at
Elmira were very much like the ones that came out of
Andersonville, except there were barracks for the captured soldiers, or at least tents. But the ground was
sloppy and swampy; the place was overcrowded; the
food was bad; the medical attention was very sketchy;
and the guards were overbearing.

The prison camps in the Civil War were inhuman.
They killed a great many young men, and yet the trouble
was not the malevolence of the people who ran the
camps at all. With very few exceptions, like perhaps
Wirz at Andersonville, the men in charge of the camps
did the best they could. They tried to take care of the
men who were sent to them. The big trouble was that in
North and South alike, as far as the authorities were
concerned, the prison camps came last. They got what
was left over when all of the other needs had been met.
They were last on the line for food supplies, for medical
supplies, for doctors, for housing, for clothing, for
guards, for all of the things that are needed to run a
prison camp. It was a matter of inattention, inefficiency, and apparently an inability on the part of either
government to understand that these prison camps really made a serious demand on their energies and their
resources. The prisoner of war got the dirty end of the

stick not because anybody wanted to mistreat him, but simply because it worked out that way. As a matter of fact, even Wirz himself probably got a much sharper punishment than he deserved. He had been wounded in action, soldiering. His wound apparently never healed; it tormented him a great deal. His health was generally bad, and he was not the kind of man to administer a large place like Andersonville Prison. The guards they gave him were home-guard types who simply weren't up to service in the regular Confederate army. Wirz was worse than most, but I think that even he was punished unduly. For the rest, it was not a question of punishing anybody. It just worked that way. It was that kind of war.

Even being in your own army was bad enough at that time. For instance, in the winter of 1862–63, after the Battle of Fredericksburg, the Army of the Potomac was in permanent winter camp across the Rappahannock River from Fredericksburg. It was within approximately fifty miles of the national capital, Washington, with perfectly free access to means of transportation, and yet the army suffered intensely that winter from scurvy.

Scurvy is a deficiency disease; it comes from lack of vitamin C. Located where it was, the army could have gotten a great amount of fresh food; in fact, it had plenty of fresh food available in the warehouses, but its administrative system had broken down to such an extent that it did not have the officers on hand to sign the papers by which food could be transferred from the warehouses to the companies and regiments who needed it. So Union soldiers, in their largest home camp and only fifty miles from Washington, died of scurvy simply because the army was in such a disorganized state that it could not get them the fresh food they needed. They only had salt pork and crackers. That, of course, was remedied eventually, but a good many men died before it was. And if that sort of thing could happen to the country's leading army, which it was doing its best to support properly, it was inevitable that the prison camps fared very badly indeed.

Esprit de Corps

It remains to be said, of course, that with all the defects in discipline and training, many of the regiments on both sides had an extremely high esprit de corps. Today, more than a century after the armies existed, there is a tendency to assume that this was more a feature of the Southern regiments than of those raised in the North. Actually, that's not quite the case. Both armies had enthusiastic regiments in abundance. A regiment that was always willing to fight and that fought with a fire and a valor unfailingly got plenty of work to do and, toward the end of the war, they were cut down to a very small number.

The Southerners had the advantage, since they were fighting on their own soil. They could feel that they were fighting in defense of their homes because their homes were not really far away. They were part of the South; they were fighting in the South. That, I think, did a good deal for their morale and enthusiasm. The Northern soldier, of course, had come a long way from home; he was fighting in what often felt like a foreign country. There were a good many times when he sat down and wondered just what he was doing there, and the whole thing didn't seem quite as carefree and pleasant as he had imagined it would be when he had joined up.

In the main, both armies, particularly in the early part of the war, had very good morale. They kept this morale in spite of overwhelming handicaps; the Southerners in spite of very bad food and very defective arrangements to supply them with shoes and clothing; the Northerners in spite of very uninspired leadership and a general air of doing things the hard way. The spirit stayed high because the soldiers were essentially good men. They knew they were good men, they took pride in the fact that they were good soldiers, and they proved their right to be considered good soldiers on a great many desperate battlefields.

PART THREE

The Roads
Led to Battle

_____

The Showdown

In February of 1861, the leaders of the seven Gulf Coast slave states met in Montgomery, Alabama. Without waiting for the new Republican administration to take office, they organized the Southern Confederacy, took their states out of the Union, adopted a Constitution, elected a President, and declared that a new independent nation existed. They did not wait for an overt act; they did not wait for Lincoln to become President. They seceded before he came in, because they knew that over the long run slavery could not live with even a mildly antislavery administration in Washington.

Out of this action, of course, came the showdown. Lincoln took office in March, found a rival government existing in the South, and found that secession was an issue that could not be ignored, simply because Fort Sumter, which was held by a small detachment of the United States Army, was located in the harbor of one of the cities most characteristic of the new Confederacy, Charleston, South Carolina.

Fort Sumter was doing nobody any harm at the time, and South Carolina was not doing Fort Sumter any harm. But the people of the Confederacy took the position that the presence in Charleston Harbor of a United States fort was an intolerable aggression; that this fort had to be surrendered.

There was a good deal of argument back and forth. Finally, in April, Lincoln made up his mind to send supplies—both food and ammunition—to the fort. Food was the most important, because the people (about 75 of them) were getting very low and would be starved out in a few weeks if they weren't restocked.

Lincoln sent down a shipload of supplies and notified the governor of South Carolina that he was doing so. The Confederacy responded by calling on the officer in charge of Fort Sumter, Major Robert Anderson, to surrender. He refused, and a bombardment began.

Fort Sumter was bombarded for about a day and a half. It returned the fire, and all in all, probably 4,000 shells were fired back and forth. At the end of it, Fort Sumter was a wreck. Since the people in the fort were out of food and it was obvious that relieving ships could not come in, Major Anderson surrendered on condition that he and his garrison be transported North, and that he be allowed to fire a final salute to the United States flag when he hauled it down.

A very odd thing then happened. The fighting had gone on for a day and a half, 4,000 shells had been fired, and nobody had been hurt. Twenty-four hours after the fighting had stopped, Anderson gathered his men to board the boats that were to take them North. As he was firing the final salute, a smoldering bit of cloth from one of the cartridges drifted down to the back of the cannon that was firing the salute and touched off a charge of powder. There was an explosion and one soldier was killed. Five more were injured, one of whom eventually died. Two men were killed and four men hurt in the great battle of Fort Sumter—all of them after the battle had stopped.

The firing on Fort Sumter forced Lincoln to take action, and it was at this time that he called Congress into special session, specifying, however, that it should not convene for three months. In the ninety days he ran the Government all by himself, he called out 75,000 troops, militia from the Northern states; he authorized the enlistment of 40,000 three-year volunteers; he authorized an increase of 20,000 in the strength of the U. S. Regular Army and of 18,000 in the strength of the Navy. He ordered a blockade of the Southern seaports; he announced that the Government of the United States would invade the South, if necessary, in order to repossess the forts and other bits of Federal property which had been seized. In other words, without any authorization from Congress, he made it very clear that the North was going to fight the war, and going to fight it hard on Southern territory.

The troops began coming in and a strange wave of enthusiasm swept both the North and the South. It was as though for years everybody had been nervous, impatient, unhappy, and uncertain while the tension was building up. Now, the guns at Fort Sumter had discharged the tension.

The men from the North gathered, got such training as they might, and in July of 1861 an army was formed at Washington, command of it was given to General Irvin McDowell, and the army was sent off to capture Richmond.

This was a completely untrained army. The separate companies that went to make up the different regiments had, of course, drilled as companies. That is, an individual company could do squads right and squads left, could form into company front, could march from here to there. But they had never drilled as regiments, and none of the brigades or divisions had ever drilled as brigades or divisions. As a result, you had a large number of young men, between 30,000 and 40,000 of them, marching off to battle, possessing only about one-tenth of the military skills they would have to have when they got into action. A company of greenhorn soldiers, for instance, might know how to march down the road in

columns of fours, and then to shake out that column
into a company front in an open field. But when a whole
brigade was involved, nobody knew quite how to do it.
When the brigade then had to march across a very
uneven landscape with an open meadow here and a
woods here and a ravine there, that was simply more
than they could handle.

At the end of their march, they came up against the
enemy, which was equally unschooled, waiting for
them. The air filled with smoke and flying bits of lead.
When a brigade that had been facing east had to swing
around and face southeast, doing something they had
never done before and doing it on a side hill full of
smoke with people shooting at them, it was all but impossible. Those were the armies that fought at Bull Run.
The Southern army, I think, had a slight advantage
because, for the most part, they waited in position. The
soldiers on either side could do pretty well if they could
sit down behind a fence and wait for the other men to
come to them. They found it much, much harder to
march across a field in proper formation, go down
through a valley, up over a hilltop, swing around and
then make an attack.

The surprising thing about the fight at Bull Run is not
that one of the armies finally ran away, but that for
several hours these completely untaught armies stayed
there and fought as hard as they did. They had had, to
all intents and purposes, no training whatsoever, and
they stuck it out pretty well, trying to do something that
would have taxed professional soldiers. They were
bothered, in the end, by two things. First of all, the
Union forces attacked the Henry House Hill, were
repulsed, and had to withdraw. The one thing that was
completely impossible for an untrained army like this
was to make an orderly retreat under fire. They could
make a valiant effort at anything else, but to turn
around and march away in formation and then halt at a
given point, face about and resume the fight, was simply
beyond them. Nothing in their training had prepared
them for it; they didn't know how to do it. So when they

began to withdraw, the withdrawal quickly developed
into an uncontrollable retreat. The men started walking
away and the farther they got, the faster they walked.
They crossed Bull Run stream and started down the
road to Washington and here they encountered the
second great handicap. The battle was fought on a Sun-
day, and it was fought about thirty miles from
Washington. A great many civilians in Washington, including members of Congress and other people who
were old enough to know better, had gotten the horse
and buggy out, loaded the picnic lunch and come down
to the banks of Bull Run to have the fun of watching a
battle. You can't imagine people doing that today, but it
was the sort of thing that came naturally in 1861, when
nobody knew anything about a battle. The fields and
hillsides lining the road to Washington were covered
with civilians who had, presumably, been having fun,
listening to the sounds of the cannon and watching the
smoke and getting distant glimpses of soldiers moving
here and there.

About the time the army started retreating, it occurred to all of these civilians—and there were thousands of them—that it would be a very good idea to get
back to Washington, so they got into their buggies and
whipped up their horses, and started down the road. A
bridge broke down, the carriages tried to drive through
the wreckage at the same time the army wagons and
guns were coming along, and there was one of the
grandest traffic jams in American history. Everybody
was scared, nobody seemed to be in charge of anything,
and the retreat which these soldiers were trying to make
became completely scrambled. It was every man for
himself. Before they got through, men who would not
really have been uncontrollable if they had had half a
chance got all mixed up with the panicky civilians,
dropped their guns, and set out for Washington as fast
as they could go.

Fortunately for the Union cause, the Confederate
army was almost as disorganized by its victory as the
Union army was by its defeat. It tried to pursue, but

didn't do much better at that than the Yankees did at running away.

Stonewall Jackson, who was not then as famous as he became later, was getting a very slight wound in his hand dressed along about the close of day. He announced that if he was given 5,000 fresh troops he would occupy Washington that night. He probably could have done it, but the 5,000 fresh troops weren't available. Jackson got that name "Stonewall" at Bull Run, during the height of the Union attack on the Henry House Hill. It was Jackson's brigade that held the line, and the officer of another Confederate unit, trying to rally his men, who had been retreating, pointed to Jackson's men and said, "Look, there's Jackson, standing like a stone wall! Rally behind the Virginians." He was Stonewall Jackson from then on.

Turning Point

The Union army got back to Washington, got sorted out, and sooner or later pulled itself together. The Confederate army followed at a respectful distance, camped on the hills within sight of the unfinished Capitol dome, and waited to see what would happen next.

What happened next was that a telegram went off from Washington to West Virginia. A small Union army in the West Virginia mountains had been doing very well. It was just as untrained as the one at Bull Run, but the Confederates in West Virginia were in very bad shape. They had been struck by a sickness, they were poorly commanded, and they folded up when the Union soldiers struck them in the mountains. So the Union army there, although it was not very big, looked like a winner, and the commander of that army was a handsome young General named George B. McClellan.

When Abraham Lincoln and the War Department tried to pick up the pieces after Bull Run, it seemed to them that the one winner they had in sight was young

General McClellan. They sent a telegram to him post-
haste, told him to turn the command of his troops over
to the next ranking officer, and come to Washington at
once.

McClellan obeyed and was given command of what
was to become the Army of the Potomac, replacing
General McDowell. Then in the fall of 1861 he replaced
General Winfield Scott as General-in-Chief of U.S.
Armies, and from then on it was up to McClellan to say
how the war was going to go.

McClellan was a very inspiring and very popular man,
as far as the soldiers were concerned. He organized
them; he taught them how to be soldiers; he made them
feel like soldiers. He looked like a soldier himself, and
they were glad to cheer him when he came to inspect
their camps because he looked like the soldier they
wanted to be. He also saw to it that they were kept busy,
that they got enough to eat, that they got proper uniforms and were taken care of, that there were hospitals
and doctors for them.

As the months went on, he became a little less popular
with President Lincoln and the administration. Mc-
Clellan had practically all of the virtues necessary in a
war leader except one—he did not like to fight, which is
a severe handicap for a General in time of war. He could
do anything but act. Fall passed into winter and winter
wore on to spring. McClellan had a large and fairly well-
trained army by this time, much larger than the army
that Jefferson Davis could bring against him in front of
Richmond. It seemed all but impossible to get Mc-
Clellan to move, however. Finally, along in March or
April, the impossible was achieved and McClellan got
his army down to the area of Hampton Roads, around
the mouth of the James River. He started his army up
the peninsula of land between the James and the York
rivers. There were long delays. He was held up at
Yorktown where he laid siege to the place and apparently took more pains with it than he needed to. The
Confederate Commander, General Joe Johnston, was
acutely conscious that he was badly outnumbered and

overmatched, and he remarked at the time, "Nobody but McClellan would have hesitated to attack us."

In any case, Johnston finally withdrew, and Mc-Clellan followed without too much ardor. There was a rearguard action at Williamsburg, which wounded or killed two or three thousand men on each side, but settled nothing. The Confederates withdrew to fortified lines along the Chickahominy River a few miles from Richmond. McClellan advanced, entrenched his army opposite the Confederate lines, and prepared for the slow, methodical, but inevitable process of siege warfare.

In those days, siege warfare was a formalized operation. You advanced your trenches methodically, bit by bit, preparing emplacements for your siege guns (and McClellan had a substantial quantity of heavy artillery). When you got the siege guns far enough forward, you blasted a section of enemy trench out of existence. Then you inched forward, occupied that area, and began the whole process over again. Sooner or later, if you had a sufficient advantage in men and material, the thing was inevitable—you were bound to win. This process did take time, however, and the catch for the Union army was that the Confederates refused to grant the necessary amount of time.

Joe Johnston, who had been in command, was wounded in battle at Seven Pines near Richmond, and he was replaced by Robert E. Lee. Lee worked out an elaborate stratagem, bringing Stonewall Jackson down from the Shenandoah Valley, striking McClellan's right flank at Mechanicsville, crumpling it, and compelling it to retreat. McClellan pulled back and was attacked the next day at Gaines' Mill; Lee's people south of the Chickahominy made threatening motions and deceived McClellan into believing that the real attack was going to come there. Jackson, Hill, and Longstreet, north of the Chickahominy, continued the attack on McClellan's right flank, crushed it, and finally compelled him to retreat.

The whole battle which began at Mechanicsville lasted

seven days, and was known ever after as the Seven Days' Battle. At the end of it, McClellan had retreated down the James River to a camp at Harrison's Landing. There he could reorganize his shattered army, get new men, new supplies, and new confidence—and perhaps resume the war.

McClellan's thorough defeat in front of Richmond brought the war to its first great moment of crisis. A second army, composed largely of the troops that had been held back to defend Washington, was put under the command of General John Pope and started down overland, the theory being that Pope and McClellan would somehow catch Lee between them, and annihilate him.

The theory was quite wrong, because Lee was not to be caught.

Secretary Stanton lost his nerve, even as McClellan did, and called McClellan's army back to northern Virginia to reinforce Pope. Before he was able to do this, Lee and Stonewall Jackson struck Pope on the old battlefield at Bull Run. There was a second Battle of Bull Run. Pope was most ignominiously defeated; his troops retreated to Washington just in time to meet Mc-Clellan's arriving army. Hopelessly discredited, Pope was sent out to a minor command in the West, and Mc-Clellan was given command of his combined troops—his own and Pope's. Lee, meanwhile, crossed the Potomac River and invaded Maryland.

Lee's hope was to score a victory on Northern soil, thus persuading everyone that the Confederacy had earned its independence. He had several things working in his favor, the chief of them being that the British Government was coming very close to recognizing the Southern Confederacy and intervening on the Confederacy's side in the war. The Cotton Blockade was beginning to be very irritating to the people of England—England, of course, had a very large textile industry, which was suffering hard times from want of cotton.

In addition, it is interesting to remember that up until that moment, the Northern government was specifically not making war to end slavery—it was making war to restore the Union, and for no other purpose. As a result, a government in England that undertook to intervene on the side of the Confederacy would not be in the position of defending human slavery, it would simply be ending an intolerable nuisance, as the British saw it, asserting its own claim to cotton, and in a way, coming to the rescue of a heroic people fighting for freedom.

In any war, the armies and navies are only part of it. The people back home finally decide what is going to happen. In the Civil War, in the summer of 1862, the prospects in the North did not look very good. There had been tremendous losses both in the East and in the West. There had been staggering defeats. The cost of the war looked unendurable, and it was getting higher every day.

A great many people in the North were beginning to question the wisdom of going on with this fight. There was a school of thought, to which many Northerners subscribed, that the South would be glad to make peace if the North would stop using aggression; that somehow it would be possible to cement the country together again if only the people in the North would stop fighting and would curb the Abolitionists. Actually, in the Congressional elections in the fall of 1862, a great many Republicans were defeated, and while the Lincoln administration retained control of Congress, its majority was greatly reduced. Whether the people of the North would continue to carry the load that the war placed upon them seemed a question open to debate.

It was probably that fact, as much as anything, which led Lincoln more and more to the conviction that this would have to be an antislavery war. He needed to harness some new source of enthusiasm; he needed a new moral issue; he needed the immense vitality and vigor that the Abolitionists had displayed, and he needed all of these energies firmly harnessed in support

of the Union war effort. If he could not find some new
source of determination and enthusiasm, the war was
very likely to be lost.

Disaffection among civilians in the North in the summer and fall of 1862 was a very real factor indeed. It
was as big a problem to Mr. Lincoln as anything taking
place on the battlefields. As it happened, Lincoln was
well aware that action needed to be taken quickly, and
over the summer he had drawn up the Emancipation
Proclamation. Secretary Seward, however, who by this
time was a very loyal supporter of the President, warned
him that it would not be politically wise to issue
this Proclamation on the heels of a string of defeats.
McClellan's army had just been roundly beaten in front
of Richmond, and Pope's army had been even more
roundly beaten at Bull Run. If the President issued an
Emancipation Proclamation, Seward pointed out, it
would look as if it were a despairing call on the black
race for help, which, of course, would have precisely the
opposite effect from what Lincoln wanted. Lincoln kept
his proclamation ready to issue, but he could not do it
until his armies had won a substantial victory.

So, Lee marched into Maryland; McClellan marched
after him. McClellan had never been a man ardent in
pursuit; he was a defensive fighter. But, in this Maryland campaign, he got a prodigious break. Lee had scattered his army all the way from Hagerstown in the north
to Harpers Ferry in the south, and McClellan, who was
slowly advancing along the old National Road toward
Boonsboro, west from Frederick, was actually closer to
the bits and pieces of Lee's army than these bits and
pieces were to each other.

At precisely this point, one of the Confederate generals lost his copy of Lee's orders, which showed exactly
where all these bits and pieces of Lee's army were and
what they proposed to do next.

History turns on very strange hinges sometimes. This
is a case in point. The Confederate General who lost
these orders had used them, oddly enough, to wrap up
several cigars and, in turn, these cigars were put in his

breast pocket. At some time, this little package had jounced out.

The Union enlisted men who found it were, of course, delighted to have the cigars and purely as an afterthought, they looked at the paper in which the cigars were enclosed. I suppose the chances were very strong then that they would have crumpled it up and thrown it away, but they were just bright enough to realize that this was something a little too powerful for them. They passed it on through channels and it got, finally, to General McClellan.

Equipped with the complete knowledge of where Lee's troops were and what they meant to do next, McClellan crossed the big chain of South Mountain and moved on toward Antietam Creek, near the little town of Sharpsburg. There, on September 17, he brought Lee to battle—the great Battle of Antietam.

This was probably the bloodiest single day's work in the entire Civil War. The Union army lost something like 13,000 men between dawn and dusk; the Confederate army, which was much smaller, lost more than 10,000. At the end, the two armies were about where they had been at the beginning, but Lee was obliged to retreat; he obviously could go no farther on his invasion of the North. If he stayed where he was, McClellan, who was gathering new strength day by day, would undoubtedly overwhelm him.

That night Lee recrossed the Potomac, and went back to Virginia, in full retreat. At his leisure, McClellan followed him.

Here, at last, was the victory that Lincoln had needed. Tactically, the battle was a standoff. But strategically, it was one of the great important victories of the entire war. Lincoln issued the Emancipation Proclamation, and the combination of two things—the issuance of that paper and the fact that Lee had had to give up his invasion of the North—changed the whole tenor of the war. It no longer was a war in which the British Government could actively intervene, because to do so now, once the Proclamation had been issued,

would put the British in the position of defending
slavery, and this was something no British Government,
then or later, could conceivably do. Also, after Lee's
retreat, the Confederacy did not look like such a good
bet in a military sense, and the upsurge of feeling in the
British cabinet, which had led them almost to the point
of outright recognition, disappeared. From that
moment on, the chance that Britain would intervene in
the American Civil War was very small and became
progressively smaller.

The Battle of Antietam, which brought out the Emancipation Proclamation, was one of the great turning
points of the Civil War. Half the war remained to be
fought; more than half of the lives which were lost
remained to be lost. But after Antietam, it was a different war, and it was going the way Lincoln wanted it
to go.

High Tide

In many ways, the winter of 1862–63 was the Valley Forge winter of the Civil War, so far as the Federal Government was concerned. To be sure, a great turning point had been reached and passed, but nevertheless, it was a very hard winter for the Federal Government to live through. If it had succeeded in driving Lee out of the North, it had no lock whatever in trying to force its own way down through Virginia. McClellan was relieved of his command in November, largely on the ground that he was very, very slow about trying to resume the offensive against General Lee. His place was taken by General Ambrose E. Burnside, an unassuming and sincere man, a rather likable person, admirable in many ways, but an extremely poor soldier.

Burnside took his army down to Fredericksburg and crossed the river, where he tried to defeat Lee's army in a head-on assault against an extremely strong position. Lee, Jackson, and Longstreet had their men dug in along a low range of hills behind the town, and from dawn to dusk, every attempt the Union army made was driven back with heavy loss. In the end, the Union army had to withdraw across the river and another wave of discouragement and war weariness swept the North. Over 12,000 men had been lost.

Part of the trouble at Fredericksburg was Burnside's own strategic bankruptcy. He apparently understood only one way of fighting: that was to put your head down and go straight forward, attacking the enemy where he was strongest. The maneuvers, the flanking movements, the feints and passes, which enable a soldier to find a weak spot and then exploit it, simply weren't in Burnside's repertoire. Burnside was soon removed. He was used later in other jobs, but he never again was put in charge of the Army of the Potomac.

In Burnside's place, Lincoln appointed General Joe Hooker. Hooker was alert, energetic, and within reasonable limits, quite intelligent. He rebuilt the army, which had been pretty badly shattered under Burnside's handling. He shook up the Commissary, and Quartermaster, and Medical departments. He got the soldiers decent food, decent treatment, drilled them, reorganized them and, in the early spring at the end of April, set out across the Rappahannock to drive Lee back to Richmond.

Hooker began very well. His opening moves were extremely skillful. He outflanked Lee, crossed the river far upstream, came down behind him, and apparently was in a position to strike as the Confederate army came west from Fredericksburg.

At that point, General Hooker apparently lost his nerve. He seems to have become profoundly affected by the fact that he was up against General Lee, whose reputation alone was already an overpowering force. Hooker waited, instead of striking, giving Lee and Stonewall Jackson the opportunity to make a few moves of their own. In the end, although he had twice Lee's numbers, Hooker was badly defeated in the great four-day Battle of Chancellorsville. His army had sustained heavy losses, and he was forced to retreat north across the river. Once again, a major march on Richmond had come to nothing.

Farther west, however, the Confederate cause was going badly. General Grant, in command of a strong army, had moved down to Vicksburg, Mississippi, and was beginning the campaign that eventually would capture that fortress and open the Mississippi River to the Federal Government.

So, while the Confederate government rejoiced in its victory at Chancellorsville, it had two things to regret. The first was the death of Stonewall Jackson, who had been mortally wounded in that battle, accidentally, by the fire of his own men. Without Jackson, Lee's army would lose a little something of its magnificent fighting edge. In addition, the situation in the Mississippi Valley had to be attended to. Various suggestions were made, among them the suggestion that Lee himself go to the valley to pick up the Confederate cause there. It was also suggested that he send Longstreet, and Longstreet's Army Corps, or at least a good part of it, to Vicksburg to fight against General Grant.

These suggestions were not acted upon. Instead, it seemed advisable for Lee to take the offensive in the east. It was argued that if he again crossed the Potomac and moved into the North, the Federal Government would have to pull men and supplies away from Grant to meet this threat, and Vicksburg could be saved.

It was also argued that, at the very least, a Confederate offensive would disrupt plans for a Federal offensive that summer, and would take the war out of Virginia for a while, giving the Virginia farmers a little respite.

In June, Lee put his army in motion for a Northern invasion. Hooker followed him, trying to keep between Lee and Washington, and Lee moved carefully, giving Hooker no opening to attack him on the way.

What might have happened if everything had gone the way Lee had wanted it to go in that invasion of Pennsylvania is, of course, an unanswered question. But things went wrong, and one of the things that went

wrong, was what happened to General Stuart. Stuart
commanded Lee's cavalry and Lee relied on him very,
very heavily. It was his function, first of all, to screen
the Confederate army so that its exact whereabouts and
intentions would not be known. Second, he was to find
out where the Federal army was so that Lee could make
his moves in full knowledge of his opponent's position.

When Lee moved his infantry across the Potomac,
Stuart was supposed to follow and then put his cavalry
in position on the Confederate right flank, keeping
Hooker's army under observation constantly, and
keeping Lee informed, at all times, of the location of the
Union soldiers. Unfortunately for Lee, he gave Stuart
permission to reach Maryland by riding around the
Federal army and crossing the Potomac slightly downstream. It looked like a good idea at the time. Stuart was
very good at swift, far-ranging movements like that,
and it probably would have worked, except that the
Union army was not quite where Stuart thought it was.
When he tried to ride around it, he got crowded off the
road, driven far over into eastern Pennsylvania, and as
a result, was completely out of touch with General Lee
for between a week and ten days.

During that time, Lee did not know that Stuart was
out of touch; he supposed Stuart was carrying out his
assignment and, when he received no messages from
Stuart about a change in the Union army's position, he
assumed it was still camped south of the Potomac River.
So Lee spread his army out wide as he got into Pennsylvania; he had one corps over near York and Harrisburg; Longstreet's corps was in and around the town of
Chambersburg, and A. P. Hill's corps was about halfway between the two.

Lee was collecting most of his supplies in Pennsylvania. It was rich farming country, the Confederate
soldiers were, for once, living high, and as long as the
army was spread out and kept moving it could supply
itself in this way without difficulty. The catch was that
if it had to concentrate, it would have to seek battle immediately because when it was concentrated, it could no

longer collect needed supplies from the rich Pennsylvania farmlands for more than a day or two. It had to
be in movement and spread out to do that.

On the evening of June 28, Lee, who was placidly
pursuing his somewhat leisurely invasion, learned to his
intense dismay that Hooker's army had gone north of
the Potomac. It was drawn up somewhere near Frederick, Maryland, and again the Army of the Potomac
was closer to the separate pieces of Lee's army than
those pieces were to each other. Where Stuart was, Lee
did not know. He only knew that the Federal army had
stolen the march on him.

He also learned at the same time that it was no longer
Hooker's army. President Lincoln and Secretary of War
Stanton had apparently given up on General Hooker.
Hooker seemed to be a good General up to the moment
the fighting started, but then he retreated into a shell.
He was relieved of his command and General George
Gordon Meade was put in his place.

Meade turned out to be a good man, and one of his
great virtues was that he did not scare easily. He did not
lose his nerve when he found himself facing the for-
midable Robert E. Lee. He moved in to bring Lee to
battle as quickly as he could.

Lee, of course, had to concentrate his army immediately. Gettysburg was a handy place, about halfway
between the two extremes of his army, and it was a place
where all of the roads met. He ordered his army to concentrate at or near Gettysburg. Meade, meanwhile, was
trying to find out just where Lee was, and realizing that
the Confederate army was badly scattered, correctly
concluded that if he could find one of the pieces of Lee's
army and assault it, that would compel Lee to bring his
army together. The battle that Meade wanted could then
be fought. Meade sent a part of his troops north to see if
they could find a piece of Lee's army. By chance, the
road they took led them to Gettysburg and there the
Union cavalry and infantry collided with a large body,
A. P. Hill's corps of Confederate infantry.

The Battle of Gettysburg began on the morning of

July 1. Initially, it was a simple collision. The two
roving bodies of troops ran into each other and started
to fight. As it happened, the man Meade had sent north
with his troops—General John F. Reynolds—had been
told to report back at once if he found the Confederate
army, and if he thought the place where he was was a
good place to fight a battle, to let Meade know.

Reynolds rode up as the battle started, concluded that
Gettysburg was a good place for the Union army to
fight, sent back word to Meade, and then rode forward
to direct his own battle line. A Confederate sharp-
shooter in a Pennsylvania barn got a bead on him, and
killed him. With Reynolds dead, the battle was engaged,
for a time, without a real leader.

As the day wore on, the Union army seemed to be
doing very well. Hill's corps was getting very rough
handling, but at that point the advance guard of
General Ewell's corps, which had been over in Eastern
Pennsylvania, began to reach Gettysburg. Division after
division came straight into the right flank of the Union
army; the Union battle line was crushed, and by midafternoon or a little later the two Union army corps that
were on the scene—the First Corps and the Eleventh
Corps—were in full retreat, hastily taking position on
the hills just south of Gettysburg.

That night, they stayed there. Meade reached the
scene and, during the late night and early morning, most
of the rest of his army came up.

At the same time, Lee's army was reconcentrating,
and on the morning of July 2, the next move was up to
him. Lee was in an unusual position at Gettysburg. He
could not fight the kind of fight he had always fought
before; that is, the waiting game—waiting to let his opponent make a bad move and then taking advantage of
it. He could not wait to see what happened because if he
did, he would run short of supplies and his army would
be in a very desperate situation. He could not retreat
without confessing that the whole campaign was a
failure, which he was certainly not ready to do.

He decided to attack Meade then and there.

Longstreet objected, saying that the Federal position was too strong, and urged Lee to move south around Meade's left flank and take him in the rear. As a matter of fact, that would have been a good move. It was the thing Meade was afraid that Lee would do, but there was no way on earth for Lee to know this. He still did not have Stuart with him, and he did not know where all of Meade's army was. He knew that some of it had not yet reached the scene and the chances were very good that if he made the move Longstreet suggested, he would simply run head-on into a fresh band of Federal troops and get very badly handled. He decided to fight it out where he was.

The Battle of Gettysburg moved into its second day. Longstreet's corps attacked Meade's left through ground that is famous to this day—the Peach Orchard, the Wheat Field, Devil's Den, up to Little Round Top. General Ewell attacked the other end of Meade's line on Culp's Hill. General Hill did what he could to lend weight to Longstreet's attack on the left center.

The fight was terrible at both ends of the line. Two or three times the Confederate attack came within inches of destroying Meade's army, but each time it just failed. Meade's position was a little too good, and it must be said that Meade handled his troops very coolly and got the most out of them.

By the end of the day, Longstreet had inflicted very heavy casualties and had driven Meade's left away from the ground it held at the start of the battle. But he still had not taken the two round tops, Little Round Top and Big Round Top, which anchored Meade's line on Cemetery Ridge. In effect, he had not accomplished what he had tried to do.

At the other end of the line conditions were no better. Ewell had made a vigorous assault on Culp's Hill. In the evening, he had his men charge East Cemetery Hill, where they almost broke through, but could not quite make it. When midnight came, the two exhausted armies still faced each other, each having suffered very heavy losses, each knowing that the big showdown would come the next day.

Meade had a council of war that night. His generals all agreed that Lee would assume the offensive the next day. Meade himself thought that the offensive would strike the center of his line, simply on the ground that Lee had attacked both flanks and failed, and the center was the only place left.

He did what he could to strengthen his position and Lee, meanwhile, brought his only reserve to the scene, Pickett's division of Longstreet's army corps, which had still been back at Chambersburg. It came up that night and was ready for duty.

The next morning, July 3, Ewell resumed his attack on Culp's Hill, failed and was driven off. In the center of the line, Lee formed an assaulting column of Pickett's division strengthened by the greater part of two other divisions from Hill's corps.

About 1:00 o'clock in the afternoon, the Confederate artillery opened the furious bombardment of the Union line on Cemetery Hill. Nobody knows how long this bombardment lasted, because nobody was paying much attention to time just then. The estimates range from one-half an hour to an hour and one-half. In any case, when it seemed to the Confederate gunners that they had done as much damage as they could do, the shooting stopped. Pickett's division, with its supporting troops, came out of the woods, lined up on a broad front and started moving across the open ground to attack Cemetery Ridge. The guiding landmark that Pickett was given when he started his charge was a little clump of trees that grew at the crest of the ridge. In effect, he was told to aim for the little clump of trees. In front of it and all around it there were a great many Union soldiers. The position, actually, was too strong to be taken by storm. What happened to Lee's men here was what happened to the Federals at Fredericksburg—they were storming a position that could not be stormed, manned by an enemy who had plenty of ammunition and the disposition to stay where he was and fire it.

Pickett's charge remains to this day probably the most famous single assault American soldiers ever made. It was done in spectacular fashion; the ground was all open and everybody could see what was going on. The soldiers moved across a half mile of open country, climbed the slope, came up to the little clump of trees and stone walls and picket fences that flanked it, and did their best to drive the Union army off Cemetery Ridge.

Their best was not good enough—there were too many Union soldiers there; the position was too strong. Reinforcements were at hand and the deadly rifle fire that was so costly to massed troops had full play here. In the end, after briefly breaking the Union line, Pickett's men had to retreat. Probably better than half of them did not make the trip back to the Confederate lines. Lee's army apparently lost about 7,500 men that afternoon, in killed, wounded, and prisoners.

The failure of Pickett's charge meant that Lee had to retreat. He had lost more than a fourth of his entire army, and he had no choice but to get back to Virginia. Lee was not in any mood to be hurried, however. He moved fast on his retreat, but he didn't panic. He gave Meade, who was pursuing him, no opening. When he got to the Potomac River near Williamsport, he had to wait a couple of days because the river was too high to be forded and it took time to build a temporary bridge. He dug in and assumed a menacing position. Meade came up, examined the situation and decided, against the advice of practically all of his generals, that he would assault it. But that night Lee's bridge was finished. He got his troops across the river, and all that happened next day was a little snappy rearguard action. The great campaign of Gettysburg was over.

A few years ago, Field Marshal Montgomery of the British Army visited this country, went to call on General Eisenhower, and toured the battlefield at Gettysburg with him. After considering the whole thing, the two generals agreed that, under ordinary circumstances, both commanding generals would probably have lost their jobs if present-day standards were invoked.

Oddly enough, both Meade and Lee submitted their resignations after the battle. Meade knew that Lincoln was disappointed because Lee's army had been allowed to escape. Meade thought he had done as much as any soldier could do in winning the battle and driving the Confederates back; he was not disposed to stand any criticism and he sent in his resignation. The resignation apparently never even got to Lincoln's desk; it was not considered. The Chief of Staff, General Halleck, soothed Meade with pleasant words, and Lincoln sent him an appreciative note. The resignation was withdrawn and nothing more was heard of it.

Lee, on the other hand, had written to Jefferson Davis, President of the Confederacy, offering his own resignation, saying that the one test for any soldier was success. He had not had a success in Pennsylvania, and it was only fair to assume that a great many people were dissatisfied. He would be happy to step down if the President wanted to put another man in his place. That was the last thing that Jefferson Davis wanted, so he too wrote his General a soothing letter, talked him out of his resignation, and the two men went on as before.

Mortally Wounded

By a singular chance, the day Lee made up his mind that he must retreat from Gettysburg—July 4, 1863—was the day of the greatest Federal triumph in the western theater of the war. On that day, Lieutenant General John Pemberton, who commanded the Confederate army that held Vicksburg and the lower Mississippi River, surrendered to the Northern army led by General U. S. Grant.

Not only did this give the Federal Government some 30,000 Confederate prisoners, removing an entire army from the board, but it also gave it the great stronghold of Vicksburg. Command of Vicksburg opened the Mississippi River to Northern warships and Northern commerce all the way from its source to its mouth. The Confederates had another strong point downstream from Vicksburg at Port Hudson, but once Vicksburg fell, Port Hudson had to fall also. With the Mississippi open, the chance that its blockade would cause disaffection and war weariness in the Middle West vanished and, as Lincoln remarked, "the Father of Waters goes unvexed to the sea."

In some ways, the capture of Vicksburg was a more decisive battle than the one at Gettysburg. The loss of Vicksburg was a mortal wound for the Confederacy, for its western third, the whole trans-Mississippi region, was now cut off. That territory could no longer serve as a source of strength either in supplies or manpower for Jefferson Davis' government, and the chance that it could ever be regained was too small for consideration.

The Federal campaign in the Mississippi Valley, of course, had begun long before the victory at Vicksburg. In the spring of 1862, just when McClellan was beginning to operate in front of Richmond, Grant won the terrible battle at Shiloh. He had been moving south along the Tennessee River, near the Tennessee-Mississippi border. A Confederate army led by General Albert Sidney Johnston struck him at Shiloh, and there was a dreadful, confused, rather disorderly two-day battle there. The Federals lost heavily and, on the first day, were on the verge of outright defeat. Reinforcements came up, Grant managed to rally his command, and on the second day, General Johnston having been killed in action, the next Confederate General in line, Beauregard, led the army off to the South.

That, also, was a very important battle, because if the Confederacy had won, it would have reversed the whole tide of Union successes in the valley. Because it did not win, the way was open for a determined Union thrust down into the Confederate heartland. It took a little time to get this thrust mounted. General Halleck, who was then in top command in the western theater, came down in person to take charge. He brought in additional troops and started down overland to crush Beauregard's army.

Halleck moved in a very leisurely way, and was never able to bring Beauregard to action. When the Confederate army retreated into central Mississippi, Halleck drew his army up around the city of Corinth, a railroad

junction in the northern part of the state near the
Tennessee line, to regroup and consolidate what had
been gained so far.

Shortly after that, Halleck was called to Washington
to become General-in-Chief. Grant inherited command
of the army in the Mississippi Valley. Halleck chose
General Don Carlos Buell to lead an army eastward
from Corinth in an attempt to capture Chattanooga.
General Sherman, who was put in command of a portion of Grant's army, was placed at Memphis.

For some time, the Federals more or less marked
time. Buell found it impossible, under the orders
Halleck had given him, to reach Chattanooga. Jefferson
Davis had put a new man in charge of the army
Beauregard had commanded, General Braxton Bragg.
Bragg moved away from Grant's front, got up to Chattanooga and struck north toward Kentucky. Buell was
obliged to follow him, reinforced by Grant. Grant,
having sent troops away, could not advance himself,
and so until about the end of the year there was very
little significant action in the west. Bragg's invasion of
Kentucky had come to grief in the Battle of Perryville.
After his defeat there, Bragg had to retreat to central
Tennessee, and by the end of the year, the Federals were
able to renew their advance.

By this time, Buell, whose slow pursuit of Bragg had
irritated President Lincoln and General Halleck, had
been relieved of his command. General William S.
Rosecrans was put in his place.

At the first of the year, Grant started down the line of
the Mississippi River toward Vicksburg. He moved
down overland, forty or fifty miles east of the river
itself. Sherman, reinforced by newly raised troops under
General McClernand, went down the river by boat,
landed not far north of Vicksburg, and made a heroic
but unsuccessful assault on the northern fortification at
that strongpoint. When he was repulsed, Grant found it
necessary to withdraw his own army from the interior
because his advance had depended largely on the success

of Sherman's move. He took his troops down the river, joined Sherman and McClernand, and assumed command in the immediate vicinity of Vicksburg.

The city was held by General Pemberton with a good deal of strength. In addition, Pemberton had one great advantage. Grant and his troops were on the west side of the Mississippi. In order to attack Vicksburg, of course, they had to cross the river, and there seemed no good way for them to do that. It was quite impossible to make an attack right at Vicksburg; the waterfront was heavily fortified and any troops crossing there by boat would be sunk before they reached the shore.

Grant's men tried several alternatives. They tried to cross the river far upstream, come down by water through a series of connecting waterways on the east side of the Mississippi River, outflank the Confederate fortifications north of Vicksburg, and capture the city that way. This proved impossible; the Confederates were ahead of them and had built forts along these narrow, cramped waterways, thus preventing them from making that advance.

Sherman tried digging a canal across a tongue of land just below Vicksburg in the hope that he could divert the whole Mississippi River, making it flow south without touching Vicksburg at all. This kept several thousand soldiers busy for three months with picks and shovels, but otherwise accomplished nothing whatever. A sort of ditch was, indeed, constructed, but the current was too sluggish to gouge it out the way the engineers had hoped that it would. Interestingly enough, several years after the war the Mississippi did divert itself through this ditch, and Vicksburg was left at the end of a long bayou, off the main stream of the river.

Another attempt was made to open a waterway on the west side of the river that would transport the Federal army downstream from Vicksburg. A great deal of work was done here, but it proved impossible to get enough shallow-draft steamers to transport an army down this winding waterway and that plan, also, had to be abandoned.

In the end, as spring came on, Grant took what seemed like an extremely risky step. He marched his army downstream thirty or forty miles on the west side of the Mississippi. He had several transports carrying ammunition and foodstuffs run the batteries by night in front of Vicksburg to join his army downstream. Then, he moved the army across the river, below the Confederate fortifications at Vicksburg, and marched off to the northeast in the general direction of Jackson, Mississippi.

Pemberton, meanwhile, was confused about Grant's objective. At first he thought the siege was being razed, then he thought Grant's move was a feint that would be followed by an attack on the northern part of the Confederate fortifications. Finally, he took part of his army down to meet Grant, leaving a part in charge of the fortifications at Vicksburg, and wound up trying to cope with Grant's thrust with insufficient strength.

Grant, meanwhile, had cut entirely loose from his base. He assembled teams of wagons, mules, oxen, whatever he could find on the plantations, to haul what wagons he took with him. He loaded these wagons with foodstuffs seized from the plantations, moved over, and took Jackson. He then turned around and finally met Pemberton's troops on an elevation known as Champion's Hill, which was some distance southeast of Vicksburg.

The Battle of Champion's Hill was a decided Federal victory. Pemberton was obliged to retreat to his fortified lines at Vicksburg. Grant followed him, and dug trenches of his own encircling the town on the east side so that Pemberton could not get out. The Union General then got reinforcements and sent them to the east under Sherman. This was to make sure that a relieving army which General Joe Johnston was trying to organize in the eastern part of the state could not get in and let Pemberton out. Grant then settled in for a long siege.

By approaching the town from the east, Grant had done a smart thing. He was able to extend his right flank to navigable waterways that connected with the Mississippi River. Therefore, he was in complete touch with his base of supplies again; he could receive food, ammunition, and reinforcements from the North without any interference.

General Bragg's army, in Tennessee, was unable to come to Pemberton's rescue. Bragg had fought with Rosecrans at the beginning of the year in a bloody battle at Murfreesboro, Tennessee. It had been more or less a standoff; both armies had been crippled by the fury of the fighting, and Bragg had had to withdraw toward Chattanooga. Rosecrans, at the same time, did not feel strong enough to attack him, and these two armies more or less glowered at each other from a distance, while the Vicksburg campaign continued.

Meanwhile, General Nathaniel P. Banks, now in command at New Orleans, was moving upstream. He was brought to a standstill at the second Mississippi River strongpoint of the Confederacy, Port Hudson, Louisiana. Banks sent messages to Grant urging him to send men downstream so that they could pinch off Port Hudson between them. These messages reached Grant just as he was winning the Battle of Champion's Hill. He ignored them, proceeded to chase Pemberton back into Vicksburg, locked him up there, and let Banks discover for himself that the fate of Port Hudson would eventually depend upon the fate of Vicksburg.

Grant's siege of Vicksburg lasted from late in May until the first week in July. During the first week of the siege, Grant made two attempts to break his way into the Confederate lines. His troops were thrown back with a rather heavy loss, and it was clear that Vicksburg could not be carried by assault. So Grant's army settled down to make a siege. They dug mines under the Confederate trenches and exploded them. They kept pinching their own lines closer and closer to the Confederate trenches. They kept ammunition and food from entering Vicksburg. They bombarded Vicksburg day and night, both from batteries on land and from Admiral Porter's gunboats in the Mississippi. A great many of the people of Vicksburg dug caves in the banks in order to escape from this bombardment. The troops did not have enough to eat; there was a great deal of sickness in the Confederate camp. It was obviously impossible for them to come out, and it was equally clear that General Johnston was not going to be able to come to the rescue. Pemberton did his best to hold out, but he was fighting against hunger and exhaustion as much as against the Federal troops.

On the day that Pickett made his unsuccessful attack at Gettysburg, July 3, Pemberton realized that his game was up. He sent a flag of truce through the lines, and he and Grant conferred late that afternoon on terms of surrender.

Pemberton seems to have had the idea that if the surrender that he knew was inevitable were arranged for July 4, they might get better terms, because the Northern government, happy to have such a good way to celebrate Independance Day, would be lenient with him. He was able to avoid unconditional surrender, which was what Grant had asked for in the first place. His army would not be shipped north to a Northern prison camp, but he did have to surrender it and everything it possessed. His men were placed on parole, which meant they could not serve in the Confederate army until they were formally exchanged for an equal number of Northern soldiers in prison or on parole. In effect, Pemberton's army went out of existance.

Grant took full possession of Vicksburg, Port Hudson fell in front of Banks' troops, and before long, commercial steamers were running the length of the river all the way down to New Orleans from St. Louis and the North.

From this moment on, the Confederacy was fatally handicapped. It was losing the war in the West. The way would now be open for Grant or any other general there to start moving east from the river. What of Tennessee remained in Confederate possession would inevitably be lost. From Chattanooga, once the Federals got there, the way would be open to Atlanta and the Deep South.

It was not too easy to see that at the time, and before the
end finally came, many months of discouragement and
despair lay ahead for the North and particularly Lincoln's government. But the end was fated once Lee had
been turned back at Gettysburg and Pemberton had
surrendered at Vicksburg. From then on, the Confederacy was facing hopeless odds.

Naturally, Grant's star rose after Vicksburg fell. It was
quite clear to the Northern government, particularly to
Abraham Lincoln, that they had at last found a General
who, as the expression went, "had the habit of victory." They had had too many who did not. Here was a
man who was completely reliable, who got the job done,
who could be trusted, and who always seemed to come
out on top.

Grant's victory made him not only a favorite of the
Northern government, but of the whole Northern
population. It increased the hero status he had won after his capture of Fort Donelson. In the early spring of
1862, a then unknown General, Grant, had captured a
Confederate army of about 15,000 men at Fort
Donelson, Tennessee. It was the first real victory the
Federal armies had won during the war, and it was
rather spectacular because it swallowed a Confederate
army entirely. On the night before the surrender, the
Confederate commander, General Buckner, had sent a
message to the Union camp under a flag of truce, asking
what terms he would be given if he surrendered. General
Grant sent back a very curt note, saying, "The only
terms I can offer are immediate and unconditional
surrender." He made it stick, and unconditional surrender was what he got.

He had done something that had looked very big,
and, in fact, was big. His initials were "U. S." Grant
and the public immediately announced the "U.S."
stood for "Unconditional Surrender." The name stuck
to him.

Grant became a very famous and very popular man.

Oddly enough, during the battle, the newspaper correspondents sent back to the Northern newspapers a dispatch telling how Grant rode along battle lines with a stub of a cigar clinched in his teeth. Grant had been a smoker, but he mostly smoked a pipe at that time. But something about that story—the image of a cigar in the teeth of the General on the firing line—struck the public fancy and the first thing Grant knew, he received from the North hundreds of boxes of cigars. He was a frugal man and hated to waste things, so he smoked them, and became a confirmed cigar smoker for the rest of his life.

Two years later, in the great Wilderness Battle, Grant was such a confirmed smoker that one of the officers on his staff told this story about him: At the start of the day's fighting, Grant in his tent reached into his possessions and stuffed all of his pockets full of cigars. The officer who watched him counted them, apparently, and said he had twenty-two cigars in the various coat pockets. That evening, just before dinner, Grant came back to his tent and a friend came up to him. Grant reached in his pocket to offer him a cigar and found that he had just one left. Twenty-one of them had been smoked during the day.

His achievement at Vicksburg was not at all what you would expect if you take the postwar stereotype of Grant that has been developed by a number of historians. Grant is often presented as the heads-down slugger, the butcher, the man who simply attacked head-on and won solely because he always had a larger army than his opponent. That is not a correct picture of Grant, and it is not at all the picture you get during the Vicksburg campaign.

Grant's move South along the river, his crossing the river far downstream, his cutting off of his own line of supplies and marching to the state capital at Jackson— all of these elements constitute a genuinely brilliant military campaign; quite as brilliant as the work of Stonewall Jackson, for instance, in the Shenandoah Valley. And until he had established his lines in front of Vicksburg and had regained contact with the North,

Grant actually commanded fewer men in the state of Mississippi than his opponents did. He was not relying on numbers; he was relying on nothing but swift movement and strategic insight.

There is another myth that has developed about Grant. This is the myth that says that Grant was a helpless drunkard. Like most officers in the United States and all other armies I ever heard of, Grant would occasionally take a drink. But to go on from there and say that he was a drunkard who had to be guarded by his staff and bailed out of trouble is completely unjustified. All one needs to do is reflect on two things. First, that a very careful examination of his record from start to finish of the Civil War never shows an occasion when anything of importance that he did in the military line was handicapped or delayed by even a suspicion that he had been using alcohol. He was always cold sober when the chips were down. Even the times when it was alleged that he went off on a bender were, without exception, times when nothing was happening and the General could be spared for a few days, if necessary.

But there is more to it than that. Abraham Lincoln was probably as good a judge of men as ever occupied the White House. He selected Grant, supported him, promoted him, and finally entrusted the entire war to him, on the ground that he was completely dependable. Give him an assignment and sooner or later it would get done. And that is the last characteristic you can ever find in an alcoholic.

Littered Battlefields

The last great strategic counterthrust by the Confederacy came in the fall of 1863, in the Virginia theater. Lee's army had withdrawn, following its retreat from Gettysburg, and it and the Army of the Potomac were simply sparring at long range, killing time until something significant might develop.

In the Mississippi Valley, too, things had come to a standstill. Vicksburg and the entire valley region had been pretty well mopped up, but Grant's victorious army had been split up into several smaller sections doing minor odd jobs in a military way, and it was not ready to resume the offensive. Only in central Tennessee was there action, and there very nearly came a catastrophe for the Federal cause.

Bragg's Confederate army had retreated from Chattanooga and into northern Georgia. It was pursued a little too blindly by a Northern army led by General Rosecrans. Since it was quite impossible for the Confederate government to contemplate the loss of Georgia

109

in addition to the Mississippi Valley, the government at
Richmond did what it had always refused to do before;
it detached troops from Lee's army under General
Longstreet and sent them to reinforce Bragg along the
Georgia-Tennessee border. Thus reinforced, Bragg
turned and struck savagely at Rosecrans and in the
great two-day battle of Chickamauga, he very nearly destroyed Rosecrans' army. If he had succeeded, the set-
back would have had far-reaching repercussions.
Whether the Northern cause could have survived the
loss of an entire army at this stage of the war is indeed a
question.

In any case, the Confederacy, for a brief moment,
looked again like a winner. Rosecrans retreated to Chattanooga, Bragg followed him and entrenched his army
on the hills south and east of the city. Unfortunately for
the Confederacy, Bragg's army was too weak to do
more than make a sort of passive siege out of it. It was
unable to cross the Tennessee River and strike boldly
into Rosecrans' rear; it could do no more, in fact, than
wait there for a final decision.

The government in Washington did two things. Like
the Richmond government, it sent reinforcements from
Virginia. Two small army corps were detached from
Meade's Army of the Potomac and sent west under
General Hooker to come to the relief of Rosecrans.
Meanwhile, General Sherman, with a very strong army
corps, was detached from the Vicksburg area, sent up to
Memphis, and told to move east and join Rosecrans.
Finally, U. S. Grant himself was sent to that area,
placed in supreme command, and instructed to raise the
siege of Chattanooga and drive Bragg away.

In the course of time, that is precisely what Grant was
able to do. The road to Chattanooga was opened,
Rosecrans was no longer under siege, and Rosecrans
himself was replaced by General George H. Thomas. By
the end of the fall, Grant was ready to take the offensive. He struck at Bragg's army in the Battle of Chattanooga. It was a spectacular battle, including an
assault by Hooker's men on the steep slopes of Lookout

Mountain and a greater assault by Thomas' people on Missionary Ridge, just south of the city of Chattanooga.

These assaults were completely successful; Bragg's army was routed and driven away. Grant felt that if he had had a little more in the way of supplies and if transportation had been a little bit better through the mountain regions, he could have pursued Bragg then and there and occupied Atlanta. He decided against that course, however, preferring to reorganize and wait until spring. Meanwhile, a small army under Burnside cleared the Confederates out of eastern Tennessee, occupying Knoxville.

So, as 1864 started, the Confederacy was in reduced circumstances. In Virginia, Lee was awaiting the attack of the Army of the Potomac; in the west, the army that had been Bragg's and was now commanded by General Joe Johnston, remained in northern Georgia to parry any thrusts the victor of Chattanooga might make. Farther to the southwest, around Mobile, small Confederate forces held land forts in a vain attempt to keep this outlet for supplies open. Beyond the Mississippi, a rather disorganized army under Kirby Smith was moving back and forth, trying to look menacing, but it never quite succeeded in pulling its weight. The principal theaters of war, obviously, would be Virginia and Georgia.

Meanwhile, Lincoln took a final, decisive step. With an act of Congress in support, he called Grant to Washington and made him General-in-Chief of the entire Union army. After years of searching, Lincoln had found what he wanted—a completely reliable General to whom he could turn over the entire conduct of the military part of the war, without needing to look over the General's shoulder, be told what he was doing, and help him plan strategy.

Lincoln called Grant in, gave him a free hand, and undertook to support him as vigorously as he could. Grant moved south shortly after the first of May. He took Meade's army, with Meade still in command of it,

down across the Rapidan River to strike at Lee. He encountered Lee's army in the wilderness, a big, almost
roadless section of cut-over, second-growth timber
southwest of the city of Fredericksburg. Here, one of
the most severe three-day battles of the war was fought.
Lee attacked Grant's army, caught it off balance and
almost on the territory where he had defeated Hooker a
year earlier, tried to duplicate the Chancellorsville victory. But, Grant was not Hooker. Caught off balance,
instead of retreating, he fought back. At the end of
three days, the two armies, having suffered dreadful
losses, faced each other in the wilderness from almost
the same positions as when the battle started. Nobody
had won the battle; nobody had lost it. But there had
been a great deal of bloodshed.

Then Grant made perhaps his most important move
of the entire war. Instead of moving back north of the
Rapidan River to refit his army and get reinforcements,
he moved to his left and struck south, trying to go
around Lee's flank and get to Richmond. Lee moved a
little more quickly than Grant had expected and threw
himself across Grant's path at the Spotsylvania Court
House. Again, a terrible, grinding battle that lasted
several days was fought. Again, the casualty lists were
extremely high, and again, there was no decisive outcome. When the battle was over, the two armies continued to face one another across a dreadfully littered
battlefield.

Grant moved by Lee's left once more, tried to get past
Lee and force the fight down the James River. Lee
sparred with him along the North Anna River and compelled him to make another move to the left. Grant got
down, finally, to a crossroads called Cold Harbor, close
to the Chickahominy. In the mornings, on quiet days,
the soldiers could hear the church bells of Richmond—
they were that close. To be sure, there were not very
many quiet days there at Cold Harbor. Grant attacked
again, with great fury, on the first of June and again
on the third, and was repulsed with terrible losses.
The armies came to a standstill, sniping at one an-

other across the broken country that surrounded their trenches. For the third time, Grant moved to the left, stealing a march on Lee this time. He crossed the James River and started moving up the south bank of the James toward Richmond.

By the skin of their teeth, the Confederates held Grant's advance off until Lee could get his own army south of the James. Lee dug in around the city of Petersburg; Grant dug in facing it. After a final, unsuccessful assault by the Federals, the two sides settled down to long, drawn-out, siege warfare some thirty miles from Richmond on the James.

To all appearances, Grant had accomplished nothing and had lost many thousands of men. Actually, he had put the war in the way of being won. He had forced Lee to take refuge in his fortified line covering Richmond. He had taken away from Lee the chance to make the swift, skillful moves he had always made before when Union armies tried to reach Richmond. In other words, he had pinned him down, and in making him immobile, forced him to fight the kind of fight that—given the North's preponderance of strength, numbers, supplies, and so on—could only be won by the North.

While this was happening, General Sherman took the army from Chattanooga and moved toward Atlanta. General Joe Johnston fell back in front of him, sparred, made countermoves, and the two armies proceeded down through northern Georgia toward the great railroad and supply center of Atlanta.

Sherman's hope was to destroy Johnston's army, but Johnston was too good a strategist for this. Sherman did, however, compel Johnston to retreat to the fortified lines around Atlanta, precisely as Grant had compelled Lee to retreat to the fortified lines around Richmond. President Jefferson Davis had complete confidence in Lee; he did not have the same confidence in Johnston, and when Johnston took refuge in the trenches around Atlanta, Davis made a decision that was fatal to the Confederacy. He removed Johnston from command and turned his army over to John B.

Hood. Hood was a heads-down fighter, a very good division and corps commander in earlier battles, but a poor man to entrust an entire army to. He attacked Sherman vigorously in three separate battles around Atlanta, lost 20,000 men doing it, and was quite unable to drive Sherman away.

So by the latter part of August, the jig was almost up. Grant and Sherman had positions from which they could not be dislodged, from which eventually they could go on to achieve their goals. If the North simply held on tenaciously and supported these armies, the war was bound to end in the North's favor. However, it is much easier to see that now, with hindsight, than it was to see it then.

Playing Out the Hand

A presidential election was afoot. All the war weariness that had been built up since 1861—and there was a great deal of it—was going to find expression in this election. The Democratic Party, traditionally very sympathetic to the South, brought the retired warrior, George B. McClellan, out of his retirement and nominated him for the Presidency. Against his will, McClellan drew to his support the entire Copperhead group in the North. The Copperheads were active Southern sympathizers who wanted the war ended and thought more of getting an immediate peace than they did of getting victory.

So in spite of McClellan's wishes, the election campaign, in effect, turned into a great referendum vote —do we carry on the war and support it to a conclusion, or do we end it now on whatever terms we can get?

If the people in the North were inclined to be discouraged, they had good reason. As far as they could see, neither Grant nor Sherman was succeeding in doing what he had set out to do. Grant's casualty list had been

heavier than anything the people of America had ever
had to shoulder before. He had lost somewhere between
50,000 and 60,000 men in the campaign that began early
in May. It was, in fact, a boast of Lee's army that each
man in it had put out of action one Federal soldier.

As far as anybody could see, this terrible loss had accomplished nothing. Far from being near a victory, it
seemed that the Northern cause was close to a defeat
because Lee had created one small diversion in his
favor. He had sent a small army under General Jubal
Early down the Shenandoah Valley to menace Washington. Early played the game Stonewall Jackson had
played two years earlier. He slipped past the defending
Yankees, got north of the Potomac, marched east
toward Washington, and actually had his army in camp
at Silver Spring, six or seven miles north of the United
States Capitol Building, at a time when it looked as if
there were not enough troops in Washington to stop
him. At the last minute, Grant sent an army corps north
under General Horatio Wright, and it got to Washington just in time. When Early moved out to attempt to
advance down the Seventh Street Road into Washington, Wright's corps met him and drove him back. Early
had to retreat north and west along the Potomac and
withdraw into the lower Shenandoah Valley.

There he stayed, and it seemed impossible for the
Federal troops in that area to bring him to grips. The
Northern people confronting the election saw their two
big armies held up, they saw a third Confederate army,
which had appeared from nowhere, come within inches
of seizing the national capital, and saw it, saucy as ever,
planted along the lower Shenandoah, still within
striking distance of Washington, and defying all attempts to drive it away.

Lincoln himself, about this time, believed he would
not be reelected. He wrote out a little paper one day in
his office, folded it, and asked the members of his
Cabinet to sign their names on the outside of it without
telling them what was in it. Then he put it in a cubby-
hole to draw out after the election. In this paper, Lin-

coln had said that it appeared to him at that moment that the Democrats would win the Presidential election. They were making the kind of campaign, he said, that meant that once they got into power they would have to make peace on any terms. Therefore, if they won the election, he felt that it would be his duty in the month between the election and the inauguration of a new President to cooperate with the in-coming administration so that the war might be won before they took office, because, he repeated, they would have won the election on terms that would make it impossible for them to win the war after they were inaugurated.

Lincoln put the pessimistic appraisal away in his desk and waited for developments. Just in time, the development came. First of all, Admiral Farragut, with his fleet, smashed its way into Mobile Bay and sealed off the next to the last outlet the Confederacy had to the high seas. Then Sherman captured Atlanta. Hood had weakened himself too much by his violent and almost insensate attacks on Sherman's army. Sherman continued to maneuver his troops around the flanks and shortly after the first of September, just after the Democrats had nominated McClellan on a platform announcing that the war was a failure, Sherman moved into Atlanta.

Hood retreated into western Georgia, and after pursuing him very briefly, Sherman camped his army in and around Atlanta to refit it and prepare it for a further advance. Shortly thereafter, Grant sent his cavalry leader, Phil Sheridan, up to take charge of the collection of troops that were facing Early in the Shenandoah Valley. Sheridan moved forward, struck Early in a furious battle outside the town of Winchester, routed him, and drove him off in high retreat.

Suddenly, the looks of things had changed altogether. The threat to Washington had been cancelled. Atlanta had been taken, and it was possible at last to see that Grant had really accomplished something by his advance on Richmond. It was clear that far from being a failure, as the Democratic platform asserted that it was, the North's war effort would be successful. Mr. Lincoln won the election by a handsome margin.

On October 19, 1864, Sheridan struck Early at Cedar Creek and completed the route of Early's army.

Sherman boldly cut his lines of communication and marched across Georgia for Savannah. Hood's army, instead of trying to stop him, attempted a counter-stroke, going over to Alabama and then moving north to Tennessee. General Thomas, who had been such a tower of strength at Chickamauga and Chattanooga, was put in charge of troops to oppose Hood. They tangled briefly at the Battle of Franklin where Hood again lost more men than he could afford to lose. Then, outside of Nashville on December 15 and 16, they had their final two-day battle. Hood was completely over-powered. His army was driven south far below the Ten-nessee line, and it never pulled its weight thereafter as an army. Part of it was brought back to the east, part of it simply evaporated. Hood himself went into retirement.

So as winter came on, the tide was definitely flowing. Sherman had taken Savannah. His army had needed to do very little fighting in its progress across Georgia. Nevertheless, it had torn up railroads, destroyed fac-tories, consumed an enormous quantity of foodstuffs, and, all in all, left a scar on Georgia and on the Southern mind which was a long, long time healing.

Grant, meanwhile, was pulling the lines tighter and tighter around Lee at Petersburg and in front of Rich-mond. Early was no longer available to distract and draw troops away from him. Obviously, when spring came, Grant would move in to finish matters. With the destruction of Hood's army, there was no place that the Confederacy would be able to make a counterstroke. The troops west of the Mississippi were too far away, too disorganized, and too poorly supported. Around Mobile, a Federal army had laid siege to the forts and would clearly capture them before long.

Sherman continued to move up toward the Carolinas. His men had treated Georgia rather roughly on their march to the sea. They treated South Carolina even worse. To a man, these Northern soldiers were not well disciplined and were used to sacking farms and towns as they came to them. Since they believed that South Carolina had started the war they felt that anything bad that happened to the people of South Carolina was no more than they deserved. They acted accordingly. Columbia, the capital city, was burned. A great many smaller places were burned. Plantations that lay in the army's path were ruthlessly looted. Charleston escaped this kind of damage because Sherman never went into it. Instead, he moved inland and cut the props out from under the city. In the end, Charleston surrendered to a navy-born expedition which simply steamed up the harbor and landed troops at the battery.

By early spring, Sherman had left South Carolina and was crossing North Carolina. He was getting very close to Richmond. Mobile had finally fallen. A separate army had gone down the North Carolina coast and had captured Fort Fisher, which guarded the entrance to the river leading to Wilmington. This was the last port to which blockade runners could come with supplies for the Confederacy. When Fort Fisher fell, the Confederacy was completely sealed in. Its last hope of getting supplies from the outside world was gone.

In its final weeks, actually, the Confederacy attempted to do something that would have been quite incomprehensible if it had been suggested earlier. It decided to enlist and arm slaves in its army. This, of course, went directly counter to everything the Confederacy was based on and would have to mean an end to slavery. If you enlist a man in the army and have him fight for his country, it follows that he has a country and is not a slave. Here was the final confession that the foundations upon which the Confederacy had been built were being destroyed.

Actually, nothing came of this move. A very, very few slaves were rounded up, put into uniform, and given a certain amount of drill in and about Richmond. They never got into action anywhere. The war ended before there could be a test of this strange new military instrument that the Confederacy was trying to form.

When spring came, Lee made his last attempt to take Grant's line in front of Petersburg with an attack on the Union's Fort Stedman. The attack failed. Grant redressed his line, formed a mobile corps on his extreme left under Sheridan, and sent it in to strike at Lee's extreme right flank. Sheridan managed this successfully. In the Battle of Five Forks, fought around the end of March, he broke Lee's line once and for all. Lee and his army had to leave not only Petersburg, but Richmond itself, and retreat wherever it could go.

Lee's first hope was that he could get down into North Carolina and join the troops which were trying to oppose Sherman there. These troops included what the Confederacy had been able to sweep together from the Carolinas, Georgia, from the remnants of Hood's army. They technically formed an army under Joe Johnston, who was at last called back into the service.

The army was not strong enough to hold Sherman off. As Johnston despairingly reported to Lee, "I can do no more than annoy him." If Grant did not run Lee into the earth, Sherman would assuredly come up in Lee's rear before very many weeks were out. But Grant did not need him. When Lee had to leave Richmond, Grant pursued with great vigor. He got his pursuing forces far enough to the south to make it impossible for Lee to go down and join Joe Johnston. Lee could only move west in the despairing hope that he could somehow, somewhere, halt, regroup his army, find some new supplies, and make another war out of it. This was impossible. Grant had kept him from moving south. Now Sheridan, vigorous in pursuit, got around in Lee's front at Appomattox Court House, and brought him to a halt. There, at the end of the first week in April, Grant's army brought Lee, at last, to bay.

Lee's army was surrounded; they had no place to go. His only chance would have been to break his way through Grant's encircling line, but by this time, he simply did not have the strength. He had slightly less than 30,000 men and was facing three times that

SKETCH BOOK

CaD
USE ng

John B G s

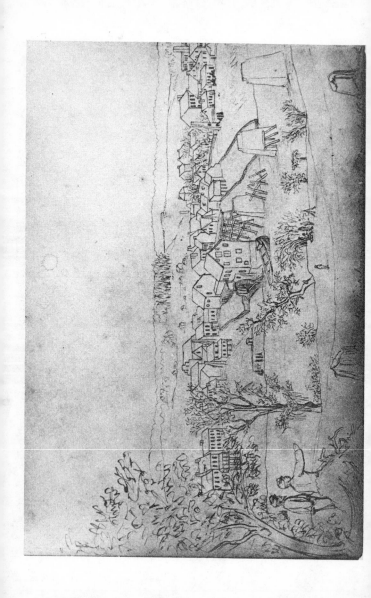

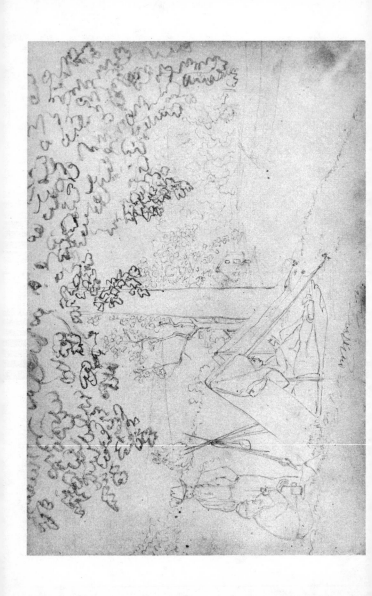

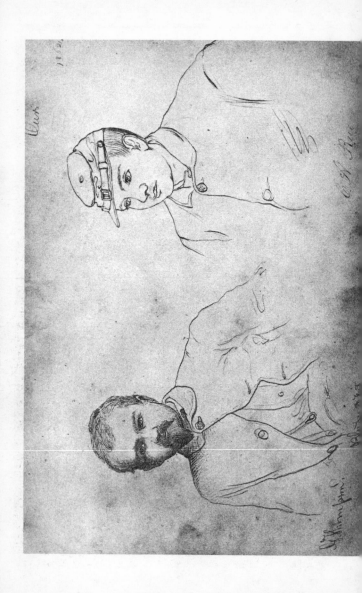

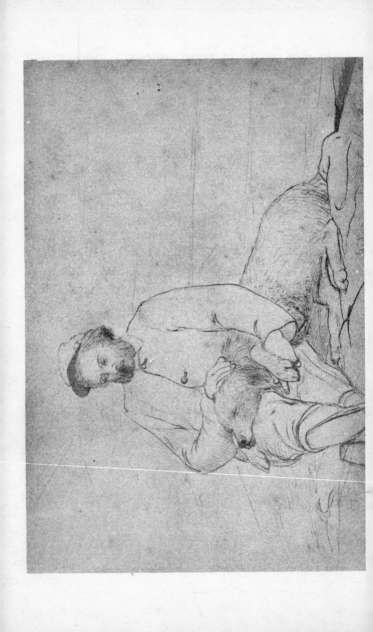

number. Of the 30,000 that he did have, probably half had lost their weapons and were simply staying with the army as an indication that they were willing to go on fighting, if somebody would give them something to fight with.

So, on April 9, 1865, Lee had somewhere between 12,000 and 15,000 armed men surrounded by 70,000 or 80,000. It was time to quit. Flags of truce went through the lines. Lee and Grant met in a little room in Appomattox Court House, surrender terms were written out, and Lee's army laid down its arms. The war in Virginia was over.

Actually, the war was over just about everywhere. Mobile had already fallen. Only a few days after Lee's surrender, Johnston surrendered what men he had to Sherman. A few weeks after that, the Confederates west of the Mississippi laid down their arms, and by early May, the war had definitely come to an end. There were no more Confederate armies in existence. Jefferson Davis himself had been captured. The Confederate government had gone out of being and the war was finally over.

PART FOUR

The First Modern War

They Failed to Come Back

Neither side in the Civil War had a program of weapons development that even remotely resembles today's. The Ordnance Department of the Federal army was supposed to be in charge of the business of finding and developing new weapons. Unfortunately, the head of the Navy's Ordnance Department throughout most of the war was an old fossil who thought that the muzzle-loading smooth-bore musket was good enough for everybody and didn't see why there should be any improvement. Abraham Lincoln, on the other hand, was intensely interested in new weapons. Any man who invented or thought he had invented a new rifle could always get access to the White House. On a number of occasions, Lincoln actually went out to a proving ground with one or more inventors to watch the new weapons tried out. He was about the only man in a high position in Washington who had very much interest in such matters, and the inertia he had to contend with was very great.

The Confederate side had not only the same sort of inertia, but a great shortage of scientists, technicians, and the kinds of people who might develop new weapons. They had some very good men; they did some rather surprising things in developing their navy. But they didn't have enough of them, and they didn't have proper manufacturing facilities. When they wanted to build an iron-clad gunboat, for instance, to defend New Orleans against Farragut's attack, they had to look all over the South to find a machine shop capable of turning out the rather long, heavy propeller shaft this gunboat needed. They had an equally hard time finding places that could turn out the armor plate that it needed.

As a result, when Farragut broke through and passed the forts south of New Orleans and captured the city, the two iron clads that the Confederates were building—which might have destroyed Farragut's whole fleet—were incomplete. One of them, a little further along than the other, had no power and was moored downstream by one of the forts as a sort of stationary battery. It accomplished very little and was blown up when the fort surrendered. The other one was still at the dock getting its armor put on when Farragut's people arrived. It, of course, was captured and destroyed.

So, the simple lack of facilities to devise and make new kinds of weapons and armaments was a great handicap in the South. The North had the facilities, but in too many cases lacked the wit to see what could be done with them.

One thing we sometimes overlook is the fact that although the Civil War was fought a long time ago and was fought with weapons which today look extremely archaic, it was, nevertheless, the first of the modern wars. The weapons the soldiers used in that war, while they are very primitive from our present standpoint, were much more advanced than the ones used in the Napoleonic Wars. They were called muskets. A musket was a smooth-bore, somewhat like a shotgun today. The

Brown Bess, the famous British army musket carried through the Revolution and Napoleonic Wars, was a muzzle-loading smooth-bore that fired a round ball and was highly inaccurate at any distance over one hundred yards. In fact it took a pretty good marksman to hit anything of any consequence at more than 50 or 75 yards' distance.

In pre-Civil War years, infantry tactics were based on that kind of weapon. If a General, for instance, wanted to assault an enemy's position, he could march his men up in the solid phalanxes to fairly close range, confident that nothing very serious could happen to them until they got almost within the whites-of-their-eyes distance. He could amass his attacking line 150 yards away and then send everybody forward on a dead run. The defense could hardly get off more than one volley while they were coming, and a great many of the bullets fired in that volley would miss the target. Therefore, if the attacking force had a suitable advantage in numbers, they could pretty well count on overwhelming the defensive line.

With the Civil War, all that changed. The soldiers still carried a muzzle-loader, but it was a rifled gun that had a range of perhaps half a mile. It took a very good marksman to hit anything at that range but, nevertheless, the gun would carry that far and it would pack a killing punch at that distance.

One could no longer get in close and mass forces before making the critical assault. The elbow-to-elbow charging column that had proved so effective in Napoleonic Wars and in the American Revolution was simply out of date. It was a good way to commit suicide. One would come under fire at a distance of 700 or 800 yards, instead of 100 yards, and the attacking army couldn't possibly run all that distance. Even if they could, the defender would be able to get off enough volleys to cut them up badly.

So the kind of attack that had carried the day before was not good in the Civil War simply because the defense was so much stronger. That accounts, in large part, for the terrible casualty lists at some of the battles, Gaines' Mill, for instance, and Gettysburg and Cold Harbor. The generals were using the old tried-and-true tactics, and those tactics were out of date; attackers who had to follow those tactics got very badly handled.

There was a much greater use of explosive shells, for instance, than there had ever been before. Furthermore, for close-range work, the artillery fired canister. Canister was a tin can, about the size of a large-sized can of tomato juice, filled with bullets the size of golf balls or smaller. The charge of powder was put in the guns, and this can of bullets was put in on top of it. The artillery piece was fired, and it had all the effect of a sawed-off shotgun. The range of a canister was extremely short, less than 200 yards, but at close range it was simply murderous. Whole ranks would be blown apart by a battery firing canister at a 50-yard range.

As a result, toward the end of the war, the soldiers themselves began to take a hand in battle tactics. When they were ordered to attack, they would spread out. Instead of wanting another man right beside them brushing their elbows, they wanted a little distance—they wanted a little room for those bullets to get through.

The wiser generals began to catch onto that and revised their infantry tactics accordingly. By the end of the war, the infantry assault was a very different thing than it had been at the beginning. Pickett's Charge, for instance—a bloodbath where 15,000 men advanced across an open field in a dense mass formation and more than half failed to come back—would never be repeated.

Oddly enough, the Civil War soldier had some excellent weapons he did not use. The Gatling gun, for instance, a primitive but effective type of machine gun, was brought out in the middle of the Civil War. It was tried in one or two places down on the Virginia Peninsula, and the Confederates who had had a taste of it, reported in awe that "the Yankees have a gun you load on Monday and shoot all the rest of the week."

But the Gatling gun never caught on. The officers in charge of the Ordnance Department in the United States Army were pretty conservative. They didn't believe in a gun like this. It was bound to break down. So they did not put any reliance in it and it dropped out of use, to be revived again only after the war.

The repeating breech-loading rifle had also been perfected by the time of the Civil War, but it, too, was very little used. The cavalry required breech-loading carbines and used them with good result, but repeating breech-loaders were rather scarce. There was one brigade in one of the western armies that, in one way or another, managed to get itself equipped with repeaters. When they went into action they had the fire power of a whole division or more, and were extremely effective. What the result might have been if the Federal Government had armed a large number of troops with breech-loaders early in the war is impossible to know. But it certainly would have made a difference.

I think a number of generals were opposed to breech-loaders and repeaters simply on principle. They believed that the soldier would get careless, that he wouldn't try to take proper aim; since he knew he could fire a great deal faster, he would take marksmanship very lightly.

There were a number of officers who simply did not want that kind of weapon issued. Also, there was a little difficulty with the cartridge. Brass was somewhat in short supply; in fact, the Confederacy could not have made a substantial number of brass cartridges, even if they had wanted to adopt breech-loaders.

Artillery, too, had developed a good deal by this time. It was still almost all muzzle-loading cannon, but much of it was rifled, and had a greater range than anything that had been used before. There was a British company, Whitworth, that made breech-loading artillery and a few of these guns were bought by both sides in the Civil War. They had a range of four or five miles and were highly accurate.

The trouble was that no army had yet worked out any

system of indirect fire. These guns could shoot farther than they needed. It would be a very rare battlefield on which an artilleryman would be located on a high enough position so that he could see four or five miles. They had not yet worked out the kind of system that became commonplace fifty years later, of advance observers with field telegraph lines sending back spotters' reports to the man at the gun.

As a result, long-range artillery never played the part that it might have in the Civil War, not because the armies didn't have such weapons, but because they had really no very good way to make proper use of them. A gun with much shorter range, one that was lighter and could be handled more easily, was much better for their purposes.

The shells fired by the artillery were not nearly as powerful as the ones used today; that is, the explosive they contained was not as strong. They were effective enough, but the chief trouble was that the fuses were very uncertain. An artillerist might set his fuse for a certain range, but he was never really sure just where or even whether it would go off.

For most of the war, the Union army had a firm rule forbidding artillery to fire over the heads of its own infantry simply because with the defective fuses, a certain number of shells would burst prematurely and some of its own infantry would get killed.

Cavalry, of course, had had its day as a combat unit by the time of the Civil War. In the earlier days, cavalry charged infantry quite boldly and very effectively. One of Napoleon's climactic charges at the Battle of Waterloo saw mounted men attacking infantry. The defense against that was for the infantrymen to form a hollow square facing four different directions, with the front rank kneeling down and the butt of the rifle placed against one foot, the bayonet pointing upward at an angle of 45°. A second row stood erect just behind them with bayonets and also with loaded muskets. The cavalry could never quite break through a square like that if those who manned the square were properly disciplined. The horses could not get past that hedge of bayonets and, while they were trying, the standing rank in the rear could pepper them with bullets.

To get around that, the cavalry in a number of cases had taken to using lances, which were long enough so that the cavalrymen riding up to a bristling hedge of bayonets could reach farther than the man with the bayonet could reach, and could spear him.

There were one or two efforts to use lances in the Civil War. During the Seven Days' Campaign, for instance, a regiment of Pennsylvania cavalry was armed with lances, but the lances were not very useful and the cavalrymen finally threw them away and relied on revolvers. The use of the long-range infantry musket meant that a cavalry charge, like an infantry charge, could be cut to pieces before it got to close quarters. It was no longer necessary to form a hollow square to repel the cavalry charge; the infantry could simply start shooting at a target that was too big to miss.

As a result, the war was not very old before cavalry gave up trying to attack infantry in position. Cavalry was useful for scouting, skirmishing, for forming a screen around the army, and if a battle ended in decisive victory and the opposing troops were running away helter-skelter, cavalry could, of course, make it much worse by riding in among them. But it was no longer a first-rank combat arm. This irritated them considerably, because cavalry was always supposed to be the aristocratic arm—one got more kudos by being in the cavalry than by trudging around in the infantry. An old saying at West Point, for instance, came in the form of a question and answer routine. The question was, "What is the purpose of cavalry on the battlefield?" And the answer is, "It is to lend tone to what would otherwise be a vulgar brawl."

The infantry took a sardonic pleasure in the fact that cavalry was no longer top dog on the battlefield. In fact, they had various ways of expressing their feelings about it. One was the contemptuous remark, "Whoever saw a dead cavalryman?" When a foot soldier uttered this in

front of a cavalryman, of course, there was an immediate fist fight. But it was a very common remark.

Also, when an army was on the march, it was pre-
ceded by a screen of cavalry that was supposed to find
out where the enemy was. The cavalry would skirmish
with the advance elements of the opposing force, and
when they had discovered what the layout of the land
was, they would retire and the infantry would come forward to do the fighting. The infantrymen certainly
noticed this immediately, and when they were marching
up to a battlefield and saw the horsemen trotting to the
rear, the foot soldiers would say, quite loudly, "It must
be we're gonna have a fight; I see the cavalry's all goin'
to the rear!"

So although they still considered themselves the
glamour boys, cavalry status declined sharply during the
Civil War. To be romantic, you had to be on a horse.
Oddly enough, that attitude never really took hold in
the North, and most cavalry regiments in the North
were recruited from city boys, rather than from farm
boys, who knew all about horses. There was good
reason for that. The farm boy knew that a horse was a
great deal of trouble to take care of. He has to be cur-
ried, he has to be fed and watered, you have to put his
harness on him and take it off, and in general take a
good deal of time to look after him. And while some of
the city boys joined the cavalry on the theory that it was
better to ride to work than to walk, the country boy was
likely to say, "No, I don't want to have to take care of
any horses," and he would join the infantry.

In the South, it was a little different. The business of
prestige accruing to the rider was stronger there than it
was in the North. Also a great many Southerners grew
up so much at home in the saddle that they made match-
less cavalry. In the long run, however, neither the
Southern cavalry nor the Northern cavalry could cope
with trained infantry firing modern weapons.

For a brief time during the Civil War—the winter

and spring of 1862—the United States Army had what you might call an Air Force. There were no airplanes, of course, but there were balloons—hydrogen balloons. They were used on the peninsula in McClellan's army as a means of getting the lay of the land and spotting the position of the enemy. One of the positive features of balloons was that it was not possible to do very much in the way of shooting them down, because there was no high-angle artillery. The ordinary cannon could be elevated just so much, and that was that. So once the balloon was well aloft, it was almost impossible to shoot it. Also, the Confederates later testified that seeing those balloons aloft caused them to go to a great deal of trouble to use concealed roads and to keep the men under cover in the woods, and for that reason they considered the Federal balloons a real handicap.

On the negative side, the reports that came down from the aeronauts were not always very exact; they had a way of misjudging what they saw and of failing to see what they should have seen. In the end, about the time of the Battle of Chancellorsville, the Union high command decided that the balloons were just more trouble than they were worth and gave up using them.

The Confederates had one balloon in front of Richmond. They were hard put to get silk out of which to make the balloon, but were finally able to find enough—in the form of dress silk from Savannah—to make one balloon. It went triumphantly aloft, only to break adrift and come down to wreck itself in a woodland somewhere. So the Confederacy's one attempt to have an air force ended in failure, but judging by the results on the Northern side, the Southerners missed very little that way.

A New Chapter

In any discussion of the Civil War, it is always stated that the blockade imposed upon the Confederacy was one of the decisive factors. At the same time, paradoxically, we tend to overlook the important part played by the U. S. Navy, both in terms of the development that took place in naval weapons during the war, and the extent to which the armies were finally dependent upon the warships and seapower.

The most spectacular naval event of the war, of course, was the duel between the *Monitor* and the *Merrimack*. This was one of the strangest fights in all of naval history. Both warships were completely experimental; nothing like either one had ever been seen before. The Southerners' *Merrimack* had been a wooden cruiser, a steam-powered frigate. When the United States Navy evacuated the Norfolk Navy Yard in the spring of 1861, the *Merrimack* was burned to the water's edge and sunk. The Confederates raised the hulk, shaved off the charred upper portion, built a citadel on the hull with slanting, iron-plated sides, mounted guns in it, and sent it forth to do battle.

The *Merrimack* was invulnerable to any ordinary weapons carried by United States warships in that day. At the same time, she was spectacularly unseaworthy. She could not go out into the open ocean; she could only cruise in calm and protected waters, like the James River and Hampton Roads. She moved very, very slowly; it took her a half an hour to turn around. All in all, she was a monstrosity, *except* for the fact that none of the traditional warships in any navy could stand up to her in the fight.

In a different way, the *Monitor* was equally experimental. It had a long, raftlike hull almost level with the water, heavily armored, and a strongly armored revolving turret on top of it. Like the *Merrimack*, the *Monitor* was not very seaworthy. She too was slow. When she did attempt to go outside the capes into the open ocean, she was usually towed by a more conventional warship. She almost sank on her way down from New York to Hampton Roads in a storm and, a year later, she did founder off Cape Hatteras in a gale. Her place, like the *Merrimack's*, was in protective waters and, like the *Merrimack,* she was completely invulnerable to anything a wooden warship could do.

The *Monitor* and the *Merrimack* got together on a March morning in the spring of 1862 for a duel. They could not do each other any serious damage. They pounded away for a couple of hours, but neither one was able to inflict very much harm on the other. Although the fight was technically a draw, in a strategic sense, the *Monitor* won it. Until the *Monitor* appeared, there had been no way to keep the *Merrimack* from going anywhere she chose to go in Hampton Roads or any of the rivers feeding into Chesapeake Bay. In the *Monitor*'s presence, however, the *Merrimack* was stymied, confined to the area around the Norfolk Navy Yard. When the Confederates were obliged to evacuate the seaward part of Virginia later that spring, and had to give up the Norfolk Navy Yard as a result, the *Mer-*

rimack had to be destroyed. She could not go out into
the open ocean; she drew too much water to go up the
river to Richmond.

Meanwhile, she had served her purpose and the two
ships together had opened a new chapter in world naval
history. Bear in mind, they were not the first ironclads
that were ever built. The British had one ironclad
warship in commission at the time, and several more
under construction. The French Navy had also built and
put into operation an ironclad and was building more.
So, the *Monitor* and the *Merrimack* were, by no means,
the world's first ironclads. The important thing is that
their fight with each other was the first battle between
ironclads.

The day before, the *Merrimack* had engaged several
wooden warships of the United States Navy. She sank
the *Cumberland* and the *Congress* without difficulty,
and proved herself totally invulnerable to anything they
could do to her. She proved, in other words, that
wooden warships were out of date, that the day of the
armored ship had come. The engagement with the
Monitor the next day simply underlined this fact.

The immediate usefulness of these two ships to the
Confederate navy and the United States Navy was
limited. The *Merrimack* did not survive the spring; the
Monitor foundered in the open ocean some months
later. Yet, the navies, particularly the Federal navy,
played a dominant part in the war, even though
sometimes what they did was not immediately visible.

Inland, the war was conditioned by the rivers: the
Mississippi, the Cumberland, the Tennessee, and
others. Armies either moved up and downstream along
these rivers or had to cross them. Control of the rivers,
therefore, was of great importance. Here, the Federal
navy got an advantage over the Confederate navy which
it never gave up. It built ironclad gunboats to operate on
the western rivers, particularly the Mississippi. These
were not heavily armored, and a few times when they
engaged shore fortifications, as they did at Fort
Donelson in the spring of 1862, they were badly shot up

with heavy casualties. But they were invulnerable to anything the Confederacy had afloat on any river. A working gunboat simply could not stand up to them, and they were largely responsible for the fact that the Federal armies in the west could go more or less where they chose, regardless of anything the Confederates had afloat anywhere off salt water. The advance down the Mississippi, the advance up the Tennessee, in fact the whole network of operations by which the Federal Government at last won control of the great Mississippi Valley and finally of the trans-Allegheny region as a whole, depended to a large extent on these ironclad gunboats that the government had afloat.

On salt water, the Confederacy built some ironclads in addition to the *Merrimack*. They had one called the *Albermarle* in the Carolina sound, which was very effective for a while.

The *Albermarle* frustrated two or three Federal attempts to get gunboats into the inner recesses of the Carolina sounds. It was finally destroyed when a brave, young naval officer, Lieutenant William Cushing, took a steam launch with a torpedo on the end of a spar, crept up the river at night, and drove the torpedo under the hull of the ship.

They had another one, the *Tennessee*, at Mobile Bay. The *Tennessee* finally came to destruction when Farragut's entire fleet surrounded it and hammered it until its steering apparatus gave way, and it was unable to fire its guns. It could only surrender. It was not sunk; its iron walls were not penetrated. It was simply pounded until it could fight no longer.

In retaliation for these losses, the Confederates at Charleston invented a submarine. It was an extremely primitive affair; there were no internal combustion engines at the time, so this submarine was propelled by a group of sailors who turned cranks, bending over inside the cigar-shaped hull, to drive the propellor. The sub towed behind it a mine, or a torpedo, as they called them in those days, at the end of a rope. It cruised out toward the Union fleet lying off the entrance to

Charleston Harbor, and attempted to dive under one of the cruisers, towing this torpedo behind it. The plan was that the torpedo would explode when the submarine got beyond range.

The submarine sank three times, each time killing its entire crew. The fact that each time it was raised, brought back to harbor and remanned, indicates that there were some extremely brave men in the Confederate navy. In any case, on its final expedition, this submarine did sink a Union cruiser. It went down itself in the attempt and, after that, was finally abandoned. But in spite of the failures, it was the first submarine to sink an enemy warship.

The principal place where the Navy exerted itself most effectively was the blockade. The blockade runners depended on their speed to escape; they were actually merchant ships and not warships at all. Therefore, any floating craft that carried guns could serve on the Union blockade. In the end, the Union government had a large fleet of armed cruisers covering all of the Confederate ports, and they exerted a constricting pressure that finally helped throttle the Confederacy to death.

The fall of the last Confederate seaport, Wilmington, early in 1865, was the beginning of the end. After Wilmington fell, there was no port through which the Confederates could receive supplies from overseas. Once they were unable to do that, the jig was up.

A Terrible Price

I don't suppose any country ever made war without making some very large mistakes affecting the duration and, in some cases, even the outcome of the war. The two governments that made war in the United States between 1861 and 1865 were like all other governments, and they made their share of mistakes.

It has been argued, and I think there is some point to it, that the Federal Government put altogether too much emphasis on the campaign in Virginia and did not throw enough weight behind the campaign in the West or along the Atlantic Coast. At the beginning of the war, for instance, the government had made a very fair beginning at closing off the Atlantic coastline, particularly in the Carolinas. It broke its way into the Carolina sounds, occupied various Confederate forts at the entrance to the sounds, took over Port Royal in South Carolina as a coaling and supply base for the blockading of fleets, and in general made enormous strides toward sealing off the Confederacy from the outside world.

It seems quite clear now that Union forces had an excellent chance to move inland from the places it had seized along the coastline and seriously disrupt the operations of the entire Confederacy. They could have cut off, without too much difficulty, the railroads leading from the Deep South to Richmond, and could probably have occupied Georgia two or three years ahead of schedule. They could have left the Confederate Government in Richmond profoundly handicapped and probably, or at least possibly, could have shortened the war substantially by making less of an effort to seize Richmond and more of an effort to cut the main lines of communication and production in the deeper South. But the Union forces did not do these things. They attempted to seize Richmond head-on, ran into the Confederacy's best generals and best army, and paid a terrible price in blood and suffering for the attempt thus made.

It was the same way in the west. They made great strides, but could have made them earlier and gone farther with them. From the very beginning, Lincoln wanted to plant an army in east Tennessee, where there was strong Unionist sentiment. None of his generals in the West would agree that this made sense, and as a result, it was not done until late in 1863. Its effect, when it finally was done, was precisely what Lincoln had expected. It opened the Deep South to invasion, led directly to Sherman's march on Atlanta, and was actually the beginning of the end for the Southern Confederacy. The step might have been taken a couple of years earlier; it was not, because military opinion ran counter to President Lincoln's opinion.

In the same way, the Southern Confederacy made a number of mistakes. It tried to hold too much territory with too few men. Its obvious course, as we can see now, was to concentrate all of the manpower it had in one or two armies, let the Federals occupy undefended Southern territory if they chose to do so, and try to beat

them on the field of battle, confident that victory there
would ultimately mean evacuation by the Federal armies
of any Southern soil they had occupied. Unfortunately
for the Confederacy, the pressure against doing that
sort of thing was too great for any government to
withstand; the territories which would have been thrown
open to Federal occupancy were inhabited by highly
vocal citizens who did not want foreign armies coming
in among them. The mere suggestion that they would be
deprived of their defenders caused them to exert a
pressure which the Confederate government in Richmond was never quite able to resist.

In the same way, in 1864, when Sherman's army
was moving down into Georgia and trying to capture
Atlanta, the Confederate commander there, the wise
Joe Johnston, understood the value of delay. He understood that the presidential election was going to take
place in the North in the fall; that a great deal of war-
weariness existed there; and that many, many people in
the North were concluding that the war was a failure.
Whether that war-weariness would affect the outcome
of the war would depend very largely upon the result of
the presidential election. Obviously, if President Lincoln were reelected, there would be no quick and easy
peace, no withdrawal. It was equally obvious that President Lincoln was apt to be defeated, if the voters of the
North continued, by election day, to feel that their best
efforts were failing and that the South could not really
be defeated.

So, Joe Johnston, opposing Sherman, took great
pains to avoid a decisive battle. He wanted to string
things out until after the presidential election early in
November. To do this, he retreated. He refused to enter
into an all-out fight, and to the authorities in Richmond, including President Davis, it seemed that he was
too reluctant to fight, that he was letting Sherman have
his own way altogether too much, and that it would be
better to make a real fight out of it. As a result, the Confederate government removed General Johnston and
put General John B. Hood in his place.

Hood, as we have seen, was a slugger, a good heads-down soldier, a man who liked to fight. But his strategic abilities were quite limited. Hood immediately provoked the showdown fight that Johnston had so carefully avoided. He provoked three of them, as a matter of fact. The first big battle was at Peachtree Creek; the second one, which is known as the Battle of Atlanta, was a little farther east; and the third one was down on the western side of Atlanta at Ezra Church.

Hood lost all three battles, and the Confederacy lost some 20,000 men fighting those battles. Because of these battles, Hood's army was obliged to evacuate Atlanta. Just as war-weariness in the North was at its worst, suddenly this long, costly campaign of Sherman's had become a success. The stronghold of Atlanta had been taken, and the people in the North took heart and began to see that, instead of losing the war, they were coming very close to final victory.

I think the decision to replace Johnston with Hood was probably the single largest mistake that either government made during the war. In the crucial days near the end, it had a direct bearing on the final result.

Bound Together

_____

One of the oddest things about the American Civil War was the fact that the two countries that were trying their best to destroy each other—the Southern Confederacy and the Federal Union—discovered very soon that they couldn't possibly get along without each other. They were bound together by economic ties that were too strong to be broken even by the stress of war. This showed itself most visibly in the matter of trading with the enemy, as we would now call it, and the war probably would have ended a year or two sooner if there had been no mutual trade with the enemy on either side.

Even while trying to suppress the Confederacy, the people of the North still needed some of the products the Confederacy supplied: cotton, chiefly, but also sugar, rice, and tobacco. The Confederacy, trying to pull away and prove its own independence, found itself entirely unable to do that without the help of things it could get from the North; all kinds of manufactured goods, and above all, machinery, leather goods, cloth-

ing, medicines, surgical instruments, pork, and corn.
Although the Confederacy was an agricultural nation, it
concentrated so heavily on such staples as cotton and
sugar that it needed to import corn and pork in order to
feed itself and its slaves. Then, of course, the Confederacy also had to have salt, which came from the
North. In those days, there was very little refrigeration,
practically nothing in the way of artificial refrigeration
or refrigerated warehouses. So to preserve meat, it had
to be salted. Without it, the government couldn't feed
its working people, whether they were slave people or
free laborers.

Due to this mutual dependency, the two sides began
to trade with each other. This became visible as soon as
the Northern armies established themselves anywhere in
the South. At Nashville, for instance, which was one of
the first important Southern cities to be occupied by
Northern troops, a very thriving trade developed within
two months of Northern occupation. The price of cotton went up to $100 a bale, and it was paid for in cash,
usually in gold or silver. That was easily two and one-
half times the price at the start of the war, and as the
war continued, it went even higher. At the same time,
Nashville was a depot through which Northern manufactured goods went South. A little later, when Memphis was occupied, this trade increased. General Sherman, who was in command at Memphis for some time,
did his best to break up the trade and found it impossible. Noticing that most of the stuff that went South
came down from Cincinnati, he declared, "Cincinnati
furnishes more contraband goods than Charleston, and
it has done more to prolong the war than the whole state
of South Carolina." Sherman was a little outspoken
and given to exaggeration, but there is no question that
a great many Northern merchants made money selling
goods to the South.

A good way to show how this mutual trade with the
enemy worked is to take a look at New Orleans, which
was occupied by Federal troops in the spring of 1862. A

sack of salt there could be bought for $1.25. A New Orleans merchant getting salt at that price would try to get it across Lake Pontchartrain, to Confederate territory. Once he got this $1.25 bag of salt across the lake, he could sell it for anything between $60 and $100. With this profit he could buy cotton at ten to twenty cents a pound. If he could then get the cotton back to New Orleans and send it North, he could get from $.60 to $1.00 a pound for it.

Profits like those are so fantastically high that no government that ever existed could break up a trade based on them. There simply wasn't any way to do it. A merchant could lose half a dozen cargoes, get one through, and make more money than he would normally have made in five years. To a certain extent, the governments unofficially winked at much of this trade. In public, of course, they announced that the trade was bad and must be suppressed. Underneath, they were willing to see a certain amount of it continue. The Northern government, for instance, needed cotton to make tents and sails for its navy and merchant ships. It also needed cotton for the mills of New England, and it was willing to pay for this cotton by permitting a certain amount of contraband to go South.

The South, on the other hand, had to have some of the manufactured goods it could get only in the North, and repeatedly, both in Virginia and the Mississippi Valley, the Confederate authorities quietly saw to it that enough cotton was sent North to enable the Confederate army to supply itself with the things it had to have.

This went on throughout the war. In 1864 a Congressional committee looking into these matters remarked that occupied New Orleans—that is, New Orleans with the Federal troops in it—had helped the Confederacy more than any of the Confederacy's own seaports except Wilmington, North Carolina.

The navy, of course, did its best to keep an air-tight blockade. It was not always successful. Indeed, even when the blockade was most effective, a fairly substan-

tial number of ships got through. It was the very nature
of the business. The North simply couldn't make the
blockade airtight.

One of the great ports for blockade runners was
Matamoros in Mexico, at the mouth of the Rio Grande,
just across from Brownsville, Texas. It was perfectly
legal for ships to go to Matamoros; Mexico was a
neutral country and the navy could not blockade that
port. Everyone knew, of course, that most of the stuff
that went to Matamoros quickly crossed the Rio Grande
and got into Texas and farther up into the Confederacy.
The navy men who had to keep an eye on this trade
noticed that a very large number of the ships that sailed
into Matamoros with contraband goods for the Confederates hailed from New York. Quite openly they were
New York owned, manned with Northerners, and carrying cargoes loaded in New York.

Economically, the Civil War wore heavily on the people
who stayed home, the way all wars do. It rested on them
much more heavily in the South, however, than in the
North. In the South, as was mentioned, there were
genuine shortages—shortages of manufactured goods
of all kinds, of medicine, and even shortages of foodstuffs. The Southern people who stayed at home missed
the work that would ordinarily have been done by the
men who were in the army. Slaves, of course, remained
on the plantations, but the average Southerner did not
own slaves. The middle-class Southerner, whether he
lived in a town or on a farm, was under a great handicap
and suffered real hardships.

In addition, the South's financial situation was very
shaky. There was a great deal of inflation and prices
went up out of sight, so that a government worker, for
instance, in Richmond, found himself with a salary that
was worth maybe a third or a quarter of what it had
been before the war. He was genuinely in trouble, and
indeed, in the long run it was economic collapse,

probably about as much as military collapse, that led to
the Confederacy's defeat.

In the North, the situation was not nearly so bad. The
North had access to outside supplies. Its own manufacturing system was very robust. It might be hard for a
railroad to get rails in adequate quantity, for a farmer
to get all of the tools he needed, for builders to get all
the supplies they wanted, but it was never impossible,
and there were never shortages of foodstuffs. As a matter of fact, the North exported a great deal of wheat to
England all through the war, and probably one of the
big reasons why the British government decided not to
get into the war was the fact that Britain badly needed
the imports of food coming from the North.

The North, in fact, had all kinds of strength to spare,
not only in manufactured goods and foodstuffs but in
people. Immigration continued at a high rate, and it was
during the height of the war that a very large number of
Northerners crossed the Mississippi River and moved
West to settle in places like Nebraska, Minnesota, and
elsewhere. There was a steady stream of immigrants and
wagons crossing the Missouri River at Council Bluffs,
Iowa, during the very height of the Civil War. Some of
the people who moved West, undoubtedly, were just as
happy to go out where the army could not reach them.
But in the main, they were just part of the great
Westward movement that even the war could not break
up.

When you study the situation of the civilians both
North and South, you can easily understand why the
Confederacy lost. It simply did not have the resources,
the manpower, the farm power, or the industry to
sustain itself. This led to widespread discouragement,
and it badly weakened the armies, which were under-
strength to begin with.

He Embodies the Cause

Jefferson Davis, the President of the Southern Confederacy, was a man who had always pictured himself as a soldier. Before the war began, when the Southern states were in the act of seceding, Davis had hoped to serve the Southern cause as a general, leading troops in the field. He was somewhat surprised, and I think rather disappointed, when he was notified that he had been chosen to be the President of the Confederacy. He apparently felt that this job would not make as full use of his talents as a general's job would have done. However, he accepted the post; he couldn't very well do anything else, in as much as the delegates of the Confederate convention indicated that he was trusted and looked up to beyond all other Southerners. He went to Montgomery and subsequently to Richmond, and became the one and only President the Confederate States of America ever had.

Davis was handicapped in that job by the fact that he had never had quite the sort of political experience that such men as Lincoln had had. He had been in politics, to be sure; he had served in a President's cabinet, and he had served in the United States Senate. But for a member of the plantation aristocracy in the South, political success in the days before the Civil War did not mean quite the same thing it meant in the North. It was not attained in the same way, and did not involve the daily, face-to-face confrontations at the level of the courthouse and the state house. As a result, Davis had never had to learn the adaptability, the skill of seeing what was on the other man's mind and adjusting to it, that was part of the price a successful politician paid in other parts of the country.

Lincoln, of course, had had extensive training in that respect. He was able to get along with individual politicians with whom he differed greatly on political matters; he could adjust himself to them and help them to adjust themselves to him. He could work with them without letting personal feelings get in the way. Davis found this so difficult, that it became impossible for him. He believed, and I think he was probably correct, that he was intellectually superior to most of the other politicians he confronted.

He was a man of very high principles, a man of great integrity, and was completely dedicated to his ideals. When people differed with him, as they were bound to do, political life being what it is, he tended to feel that they were willfully wrong and that there was some sort of moral failure in them that caused them to differ.

As a result, it was very hard for Davis to bring them along with him, and as the war progressed, a fairly substantial number of Southern leaders found it almost impossible to work with him. This included some very good generals, like Joseph E. Johnston and Beauregard. Between those men and Davis there developed a personal antagonism that stemmed from nothing more serious than disagreement about tactics and matters of strategy. It developed into more than that, however; it developed into personal distrust and dislike. Johnston, for instance, who was one of the best soldiers on either

side in the war, reached the point where he and Mr.
Davis simply could not communicate, much less work
together. I think the fault was as much on Johnston's
side as it was on Davis', but that is not the point. The
point is that Davis lacked the flexibility that enabled
Lincoln, for instance, to get a great deal of work out of
General McClellan, even while he and McClellan
privately despised each other. To be sure, they came to a
parting of the ways eventually, but before that, Lincoln
got a lot of service out of General McClellan.

Because Davis could not get along with soldiers like
Johnston and Beauregard, he could not use them to the
limit of their capacity. On the other hand, he insisted on
clinging to other soldiers much less capable than these
two, simply because they did agree with him; men like
Braxton Bragg, for instance, and John Pemberton.
They were definitely not of top-flight caliber, but because they could get along with Mr. Davis they held high
positions in the Confederate Army long after they
should have.

Davis, of course, had an almost impossible job to do
in the first place. He was President of a comparatively
small, poor country fighting a comparatively large, rich
country. The United States in the North was highly
developed, industrially, for that day. Industrial development in the South was very small and the resources
to increase it during wartime did not exist. Davis did his
best, I think, with the materials at hand, and even the
human failures that I have mentioned probably would
not have been fatal if the South had had within its
borders the industrial and economic resources needed to
wage war against a stronger power.

It rather quickly boiled down to a business of hanging
on and hoping that the people in the North would
finally get tired of the struggle and give up. The chance
to win a victory in the field vanished, probably with the
Battle of Gettysburg, but it was hard for Davis to see
this. Davis saw his entire problem in purely military
terms. His grasp of the political situation in the North
was imperfect; he tended to ignore problems raised by

industrial deficiencies and the lack of money. To the end, he hoped that one or more great victories in the battlefield would solve the Southerners' problems. That simply wasn't in the cards. Davis tried to reach out for it; he replaced Johnston in front of Atlanta with John Hood in the hope that Hood would make a fight of it and defeat Sherman. Hood made a fight of it, all right, and wrecked his own army doing it.

A little later, Davis approved Hood's attempt to bring Sherman back from his march across Georgia by invading western Tennessee. Hood made the invasion, and neither he nor the Confederate President realized that by this time, Northern strength was so great that by detaching part of his army and rallying troops from the North to help it, Sherman was able to leave in Tennessee enough of a force to handle Hood while he, himself, with 60,000 men marched unopposed to Savannah. Of course, after he reached Savannah, the game was just about over.

Hood, meanwhile, ran into General Thomas at Nashville. He was overwhelmingly defeated by Thomas, and the troops that had been left with him were for all intents and purposes put out of the war.

So the final year of the war was a downhill pull for the Confederate President, and there really was nothing much he could do about it. He hung on with great dedication and complete courage to the very end, refusing to give up as long as there was the slightest chance to hang on. In fact, he refused to give up even after the slightest chance had vanished. The final month or two of the war constituted a hopeless struggle for the Southerners. The Confederate government had collapsed, and the Confederate armies were destroyed. Davis, himself, was arrested. He was confined in prison quarters at Fort Monroe and for quite a while it appeared that the Federal Government would put him on trial for treason. A year passed and then two years, and at last it became apparent that the Federal Government was going to do nothing of the kind.

A treason trial for Jefferson Davis would have cost

much more than it was worth and would have settled nothing. There were plenty of people in the North who supported Davis at this time. Even such a man as Horace Greeley, the Abolitionist editor of the New York *Tribune*, definitely opposed the treason trial for Davis and came to Davis' support while he was in Fort Monroe. Eventually the men in charge in Washington realized that it was better to let bygones be bygones; the war was over; the attempt at secession had been defeated once and for all, in such a decided way that it would never be tried again. It was possible to see that men like Davis had not been traitors, but had been, according to their own lights, patriotic Americans, trying to gain for themselves and their people what they considered complete freedom.

When Davis was at last released he had some difficulty making a living. He worked for a while as an officer in a life insurance company. He visited in Europe for a time and, at last, he settled down to write his memoirs and other pieces justifying the course the South had taken in the 1860s. To the end of his life he did not withdraw from the position he had taken during the war, insisting that the South had been justified in its actions. He did not try to stir up a new war; he accepted the result. The attempt to secede had failed, and would never be made again. Davis, obviously, did not want to try to make it again. But he refused to admit that he had been morally wrong or that the South had been wrong. He stuck by his guns and, to the day of his death, maintained that all that he and his fellow citizens had tried to do was right and proper, even though it had failed. But toward the end of his life, Davis got some compensation—spiritual compensation.

During the final year of the conflict, Davis had become one of the most unpopular men in the South. The politicians he had been unable to get along with and the famous generals he could make no further use of had had strong followings. In 1865, when the Confederacy collapsed, a great many Southerners believed that it was mostly Davis' fault; that, with another man as President, they might have done better.

The years passed and, by the 1880s, people throughout the South had generally come to a different viewpoint. They had come to see Davis as the embodiment of the courage and dedication that had supported the Southern cause. They remembered, too, that to the day of his death, Robert E. Lee, who was by far the most revered man in all of the Confederacy, had never said a word of criticism of President Davis, that he had been able to work with him to the very end, and to the end of his life had had high admiration for the man. In addition, Davis' own writings had helped. He had traveled abroad and was received in England as Lee's spokesman for the late Confederacy.

So after enough time had passed for the wounds to begin to heal, the people of the South began to enshrine Davis among their heroes, not so much for what he had done during the war, but for the way in which, since the war, he had come to embody what they had believed in and hoped for. By the time of his death, Davis had reestablished himself as a Southern hero. He had moved into a niche in Southern affections which he occupies to this day, and I don't think there is much tendency in the North to try to dislodge him from that peculiar niche. He is remembered as an admirable, memorable American, and I think he will always be remembered as such, even by those Northerners who rejoice heartily that the Confederacy itself was destroyed. He is also accepted universally, I believe, as a difficult man, a man not easy for a great many others to get along with, not too easy to know, not too easy to love. But nevertheless, we see him as a man of dauntless courage, a man of complete personal integrity, a man of the highest ideals, who sacrificed himself and his career for the cause that meant more to him than anything else in the world.

PART FIVE

There Was a Young Soldier

———————————

The Heather Is on Fire

Follow a Civil War soldier through a battle and you find that you are studying two incomprehensible paths through space.

One is the trajectory of the bullet that kills him: flat, direct, whining, going from here to there (200 yards, as likely as not) in a second or two and then stopping forever.

The other is the trajectory of the man.

It is infinitely complicated, unhurried, wandering down through the years with all sorts of twists, convolutions, false starts, unexpected dips and curves, and meaningless pauses. There is no pattern to it. It just goes until something stops it, or until its original impetus is finally exhausted. And then it stops forever . . . or at least it vanishes to where we no longer can see it.

If these two trajectories—that of the bullet and that of the man—meet, they both end, and one who looks on at a safe distance is likely to begin an unsatisfying speculation. The short life of the bullet's flight caused it to be at one particular point in space one foot above the top rail of a fence along Farmer Jones' cornfield, say, at precisely twenty-one minutes past nine o'clock on a certain Tuesday morning in September. The man's own flight, leisurely and whimsical, and all but purposeless, guided by forces whose complexity we can never understand, brought him from afar to that same place at exactly the same moment. If any of the infinite chances by which life is guided had made him veer one foot the other way or had delayed him by one second, his trajectory would not have crossed the trajectory of the bullet and he would have lived. How did he happen to be there—precisely, irrevocably there and not somewhere else—in the fraction of a second when the flying bullet was going to be there too?

Suppose (to follow a wholly profitless speculation) his company had been two seconds late in falling into line that morning when it was time to break camp and take to the road. Suppose his regiment, advancing to possess a smoky woodlot, had swung a yard farther to the right; suppose the man himself had tripped over an uneven spot in the field and had reached the fence a moment later than he did reach it; in any of these cases, the two trajectories would not have met and the man would have gone on living—for two minutes, or for fifty years, or whatever. Suppose, suppose, suppose . . . you are beginning to touch a mystery that is beyond earthly understanding, whether you want to speak of an inscrutable fate, divine Providence or a blind bumbling chance that makes a mockery of all our dreams. There is not any answer we can lay our hands on.

In other words, the riddle is insoluble and there is no profit in pursuing it. But that does not stop us from studying the man's trajectory, because the riddle of the soldier's fate is the same riddle that is common to all of us, whether we are in the army or live our lives out in the sunny times of peace. We are like the soldier whose career we follow: There is no way on earth to know what the next sentence is going to tell us. The human trajectory is eternally incalculable, beginning in deepest mystery and going blind to a fate no one can predict.

But the business is best studied in wartime, because then we do not need to admit that the terror and the tragedy are personal to ourselves. It is possible to admit the regency of blind chance because that is what governs men in wartime, and if the war has long since been ended, its tragedies do not touch us so closely. So we consider the life of the soldier, and we reflect that it does not go according to plan. It bumps and drifts and sometimes it lies in military backwaters waiting for some eddy to take it out into the mainstream; some soldiers drift on inexorably to that final appointment while others go past it and get to the end of the battle and the end of the war with the end of life still lying somewhere far ahead. This, of course, is not to say that the soldier who survives for a quiet old age in the village sunlight, chatting about the past with a few survivors like himself, is the same man as the one who enlisted when the war was young. He has lost something; if not life itself, then the dreams and illusions of youth which once seemed to give life its meaning. He has come down to earth ahead of time.

Probably that is why our old Civil War veterans in their final years seemed so clannish. They stuck together as much as they could because they shared an understanding other folk did not have. Like Adam, they had been cast out of the enchanted garden, leaving innocence behind. This, to be sure, happens to everybody sooner or later, but the point to remember about these Civil War soldiers is that they came from a much less sophisticated age than any soldiers who have appeared since then. They had more innocence to lose, they had farther to fall, and if the actual shock was not really greater, they were less well prepared to adjust to its effects. Today's soldier ceased to believe in the great garden long before he ever left it; the Civil War man for the most part lived happily in it up to the moment when the flaming sword was swung, and he came out into the workaday world all unprepared.

All of which is as it may be, and there is not much

point in dwelling on it, except that it helps one understand the dogged survival of the irrational hope that some day men will make war no more. What is more interesting is the fact that the Civil War soldier, once the war did end, spent no time moaning about the cruelty and injustice of life (of which, by the war's conclusion, he had an abundant understanding), and he never saw himself or invited others to see him as a member of a "Lost Generation," brutally sinned against by his elders. He buckled down to it and tried to make the best of the life that had been spared to him, and he had no self-pity to speak of. But of course, he did not forget . . .

There was a young soldier named John B. Geyser. He came from Allegheny City, Pennsylvania, and there is no use looking for it on a modern map because it has long since become a part of Pittsburgh. He was a patternmaker in an Allegheny City machine shop, he was twenty-three years old when the bombardment of Fort Sumter effectively announced that the Civil War had begun, and he was one of the very first young men to respond to Abraham Lincoln's call for volunteers. The dates speak for themselves: Fort Sumter came under fire on April 12, 1861, its flag was hauled down next day, the Federal garrison was formally evacuated on April 14, and on April 15, Lincoln called on the states for 75,000 men to serve for three months. On April 20, John Geyser enlisted in the 7th Pennsylvania militia regiment, which was formally mustered in two days later with Geyser as a member of Company F. His enlistment papers show that this young soldier stood six feet tall, had gray eyes and fair hair, and his regiment went to a camp of instruction (as army training camps were called in those days) at Harrisburg.

All in all, John Geyser had lost very little time. He was one of that first magnificent surge of young men who suddenly discovered that they wanted to join the army more than they wanted anything else on earth. There will never be anything like it again. These young men *believed*, as men today do not believe, and their faith made them innocent. Their youth was a shining coin worth nothing unless it was spent, and they had the tipsy joy of spendthrifts. There were festive recruiting excursions to raise men—wagons trundling along sandy roads with officers and a band of music aboard, stopping in small towns for music and oratory, crowds on hand to cheer and to listen to the patriotic speeches (delivered mostly by portly middle-aged types who did not themselves enlist); and the torch lights flickered up and down village streets while the young men stepped forward to join up, and girls in white frocks stood around the platform or strolled down the sidewalks under the maples, somehow representing (although nobody knew quite why or how) the noble cause which the recruits were going to serve. And so the young men walked up to the platform, shy enough most of them, and signed their names and then strolled down the village lane with Sally and as likely as not got a kiss for reward; and this happened over and over until finally the regiment had its quota and it went off to camp, to put on ill-fitting uniforms and endure the deadly recruit-camp diseases and learn some of the rudiments of soldiering until the great day when the regiment was put on a train to go to "the front."

They were moved, as we say, by patriotism, and their patriotism had an intimate quality. People in those days mostly stuck close to home. They had to, because it was so hard to move about. There were no automobiles, of course; the roads were terrible and, except for farmers and well-to-do folk, nobody had horses; if you went anywhere, you rode the trains (which were expensive) or you walked. A young man stayed at home, and his fatherland was what he could see from his bedroom window, along with the few square miles he might tramp about in the area near his home. Everything else he took on faith. His America was small enough to carry in the mind and in the heart, small enough to love with a deep, unformulated emotion that was all the more powerful because it never had to be defined. He never questioned the force or the rightness of this emotion anymore than he questioned his love for the members of his immediate family: It was a thing given, a thing he lived with, and when it was stirred he did what it told him to do without dreaming of asking critical questions.

That was how the young men of 1861 knew America. They also knew, of course, the schoolbook history, the Spirit of '76, the Patriots' uprising, the Minute Men and Valley Forge, and all the rest. That had built up something in their minds. If they had been asked to define it, they would have been unable to do it; but they had a feeling for tradition, for the things brave men had done to make American life possible for them. And they had a deep instinctive bond to the home place, the country they knew and tramped over and saw with the light of summer sunset on it, or the sepia-and-white tones of a snowy field in January sloping up to a muted sky beyond the brown branches of hibernating trees.

Their schooling was fairly simple; usually the one-room schoolhouse of tradition, something better in cities and towns, but very spare and bleak in the country regions, which was where most of the young soldiers came from. There was no nonsense then about requiring people to finish high school, or even grade school. A boy went to school as long as he felt like it, or as long as his parents could afford to spare him from chores around the farm or about the house, and then he quit and went to work. He got as much or as little education as his neighborhood could give him or as he himself could assimilate, and that was that. It was a simple education, simply given, and it probably would give the blind staggers to any graduate of a school of education nowadays, but it did turn out literate people who had some understanding of what their country was all about, how it got started, and what it depended upon. It could have been better, but it could also have been a great deal worse.

So there was, in 1861, a great mass of people—like young John Geyser—coming out of their teens and into their twenties in a land that, as far as their memories went, had always been at peace. The country was growing, it was making progress, each year there were more chances for jobs, more land for an ambitious young farmer to break to the plow, and altogether it looked like a good life. Indeed, it *was* a good life, and when something happened that seemed to challenge this life, the response was instinctive and automatic. They would fight to defend this, even though they might not be quite sure what they were defending it against; they would just fight.

There is one more point to consider when the great outpouring of volunteer soldiers after Fort Sumter is examined. A great many of these young men—happy, well-fed, busily laying the foundations for lives which they knew would be good—were just a little bit bored. They were stay-at-homes. They had read and heard about the noble deeds Americans of earlier days had performed, from Daniel Boone to Meriwether Lewis to Davy Crockett, and all of those things had happened long ago and far away. Here these youngsters were, following a plow across the farm or doing a job in some village shop, and while this was nice and they wanted to keep on doing it, there were moments when it was a mite dull. There was not much excitement in anybody's life. There were no athletic contests to speak of. Baseball was just developing, and had hardly taken hold anywhere; football, basketball, and similar games had not yet appeared. Although young men would now and then have wrestling matches or run footraces, the excitement and thrills that come from athletics nowadays were not a part of their lives.

So when the militia companies were called up in the spring of 1861, and a little later when the recruitment of three-year volunteers was ordered—42,000 in the first lot, 400,000 two months later—everything went with a rush. The inbred patriotism that lived so close to the surface was enormously stimulated by a great craving for adventure. One writer expressed it simply by remarking: "The heather is on fire," and a youth who went off to training camp, and found himself leading a life completely different from anything he was used to, wrote gaily: "It sure beats clerking." War's arrival was joyously welcomed by the men who were going to have to carry the load. (Nobody especially noticed it at the time, but it was recalled later that the men who were well on in their thirties and had served in the war with Mexico did not join in the hallelujah chorus. Where war is concerned, as indeed in other matters, one can lose virginity only once.)

Even among mature folk, the war came as a release from tension. There had been the mounting discord between North and South, the steady sharpening of the dispute over slavery, the rights of the states, and the proper role of the Federal Government. Now, at last, it had come to a head and apparently an argument everyone was tired of was going to be settled. It would be settled the hard way—just how hard, people would presently find out—but at least it would be disposed of, and there was relief in the thought.

They Think
Themselves Perfect

John Geyser's experience in the camp of instruction was
unlike that of most Civil War soldiers, simply because
he got into the act so early that the authorities who had
invited him in were not in the least bit ready for him.

The 75,000 men the states raised in response to Lincoln's call were, of course, all organized as state militia.
They had to be because the government then did not
have any provision for raising and training men fed-
erally. (It did have the regular army, to be sure, but that
was commonly looked on as a refuge for drunken deadbeats, and it was thought that ardent young patriots
would have none of it. Besides, it was operating under
limits set by an act of Congress, and it was not believed
that the President could increase its number without
proper authorization.) So the government had to rely on
the states, and the rules then were that state militia
could be called into Federal service for no longer than
three months. The call for the first 75,000 was based on
a law passed in 1795, which as an added safeguard pro-

vided that Federal use of militia must in any case expire "30 days after the commencement of the then next
session of Congress" which, in 1861, had been called to
meet in extra session on July 4. Having enlisted before
the call for a special session was issued, Geyser's 7th
Pennsylvania regiment accordingly counted its 90 days
from the date it was mustered; its time thus would expire 90 days after April 24, or July 23.

A special problem faced by this and the other Pennsylvania regiments was that the Government felt compelled to use the men on active service before it had
given them more than the sketchiest sort of training and
before it had provided them with anything worth men-
tioning in the way of uniforms, weapons, equipment,
tents, or even cooking utensils. When these regiments
began to appear along the upper Potomac, where they
might encounter armed Rebels any day, a dispassionate
regular army officer wrote that "our volunteers are
green as grass," noting that they "are marching in their
fours, if they have a drum or a band . . . yet they think
themselves perfect." What the officer was getting at, of
course, was the fact that parade-ground marching—getting into column of fours and keeping step while moving
past a reviewing officer—was the least of all the things
the recruit had to learn. Until he learned how to shift
from marching column into a fighting formation, and
could do it in a briar patch or on a hillside leading down
to a swamp, with unseen enemies shooting at him, the
young soldier was precisely what the regular called him:
green as grass, and likely to be useless in combat.

Along with the other Pennsylvania militia regiments,
fifteen of them in all, the 7th was under command of
Major General Robert Patterson of the Pennsylvania
militia, a ninety-day man himself, who was at the moment commander of the Department of Pennsylvania.
Patterson was a prosperous business man of the lead-
ing-citizen type, and if he was a ninety-day General, he
had had a good deal of very solid military experience
under fire, in the War of 1812 and in the war with Mexico. All in all, he was a good man who deserved a better

break than fate was about to give him. He was sixty-nine, the bulk of his troops were so wretchedly trained and outfitted that it was quite impossible to form them into an army or to use them as an army should be used, the Federal Government found that it could not clearly tell him just what he was expected to do, and underlying all of these woes was the fact that the government really wanted him to serve two diametrically opposed functions at the same time.

By May 1 Patterson had had a look at his new command. He reported that it was composed of unequipped regiments at the camps of instruction in Chambersburg, Lancaster, Harrisburg, York, and Philadelphia. No regiment was fully armed, and they lacked tents, canteens, and cooking equipment; the weapons they bore —if, indeed, they had any at all—were mostly defective, muskets with broken locks or rust holes through the barrels being common. Troops that had bayonets usually found that these did not fit the muskets they accompanied and hence were of no use. Five days later, Patterson remarked that three of his fifteen regiments had managed to get cooking utensils, but that only one had tents. Most soldiers had no ammunition at all. As late as May 23 (one third of the time of enlistment already gone) the Frankford Arsenal was notifying him that it could issue accouterments to the 7th regiment at its Chambersburg camp "tomorrow." (Accouterments included such necessities as haversack, knapsack, canteen, cartridge box, and the like—items the soldier simply had to have if he were even to stir outside of the home camp.)

With time, of course, these deficiencies would be made good, but the trouble was that the ninety-day man had no time to spare; he was needed in action right now, and the military clock kept ticking relentlessly, moving him on toward the day when his enlistment would expire.

Not that people weren't trying. But the problem that plagues war departments and armies at the outset of every American war was raising its head: the very size

and urgency of the need makes meeting it promptly im-
posssible. As early as April 23 the War Department had
instructed the Quartermaster General to produce
"forage caps, infantry trousers, flannel sack coats, flannel shirts, boots, stockings, greatcoats, blankets and
such other articles as may be necessary to supply the
wants of the troops of the different states in service
under the requisition of the President." The Quartermaster General dutifully set about it, but between the
placing of the orders and the delivery of the finished
goods, there was bound to be a gap. At the end of April,
Pennsylvania's governor, Andrew G. Curtin, asked the
War Department (somewhat plaintively) whether the
state or the Federal Government was to provide uniforms and camp equipment. He was told that these were
always supplied by the Federal Government but that,
under the circumstances, it was impossible to forward
all of this material as rapidly as possible. Curtin, accordingly, was urged to provide these things himself and
send the bill to Washington.

Some of the new regiments, including the one John
Geyser was in, suffered from an especial handicap: they
were not built around a preexisting framework, but
were brand new in every respect, from greenhorn colonel and recruits on to the tables of organization at
headquarters. (Indeed, headquarters itself had to be improvised.) Where a militia regiment had existed before
the war there was something to build on—officers, noncoms, a bloc of private soldiers who at least had seen
each other before, and there was some sort of regimental history, a place in the state's scheme of things, a
nucleus around which a cohesive structure could be
made. After a brief time in camp, such regiments were
ready (by the standards of that age) to be put into action, and many of them acquitted themselves very well.
But the militia regiments that were started from scratch
had nothing at all, and for some time it appeared that
nobody was really responsible for them.

Curtin did his best, and so did Patterson, who by
June 1 was able to notify the War Department that he

had at Chambersburg six infantry regiments tolerably well equipped, plus four more that still lacked accouterments, and that he was prepared to obey orders promptly. The War Department ordered him to move South, "turning" the Rebel post at Harpers Ferry (which meant that he was to bypass it), cross the Potomac, and move into Virginia in the direction of Winchester. By mid-June, Geyser's regiment found itself camped along the upper reaches of Antietam Creek not far north of Sharpsburg and convenient to the Potomac town of Williamsport, where Patterson was to take his troops across the river. Patterson had been given a couple of battalions of regulars and a well-drilled Rhode Island militia regiment, and he was confident that he could carry out his mission, which in substance was to hold the upper Potomac, protect the line of the Baltimore and Ohio Railroad, and ultimately to join hands with troops led by General George B. McClellan, who was coming east across West Virginia. So far, so good.

Then came trouble.

What the War Department feared most this spring was that Washington might be seized in a sudden dash. G. T. Beauregard, the Confederate General widely publicized as the "Hero of Fort Sumter," had assembled an army in the vicinity of Manassas Junction. Although he had aggressive purposes, the real danger, Washington believed, would come from the lower Shenandoah Valley. General Joe Johnston had 12,000 men in and around Winchester, with outposts along the Potomac all the way from Martinsburg to below Harpers Ferry. (He had two lieutenants, Jeb Stuart and Stonewall Jackson; the latter had not yet won his nickname, and nobody then realized how extremely dangerous to the Union cause these two officers were going to be.) Johnston, the Government thought, was likely to slip across the river, move swiftly downstream and gobble up the Federal capital if he were not closely watched and carefully handled. The government was probably right, and that is why Patterson was up there.

Then the picture changed. General Irvin McDowell
was given an army (just about as green and clumsy as
Patterson's) and ordered to drive Beauregard from
Manassas, opening the road to Richmond. Given this
situation, it was feared that Johnston would slip away
from the valley and come to Beauregard's aid. So Patterson's assignment was changed. He was still to guard
the upper Potomac against an advance by Johnston; he
was also to look menacing so that Johnston would stay
in the Winchester area, and although he ought to fight
him, he was under no circumstances to drive him east of
the Blue Ridge. To make matters worse, the Government never managed to specifically explain to Patterson
just what he was supposed to do. He was supposed to
keep Johnston busy which, under the circumstances,
could only be done by fighting him constantly, but he
must also stay on the defense and not fight very hard,
and above all things he must not risk the danger of
defeat. An impossible assignment, especially for a pea-
green army. Fight—and also don't fight: advance, but
keep your back close to the Potomac crossing . . . and
on top of everything else the Government took Patterson's regulars and Rhode Islanders away from him,
leaving him with practically nothing except the rookie
Pennsylvanians, who were glumly aware that they were
not really ready to fight anyone, and who also realized
that their terms of service would expire in a few weeks.
They had not yet been paid, and so the majority, who
had had no shoes and could not get any from the Government, could not even *buy* shoes because they had no
money. Patterson unhappily notified the government
that hardly any of these men could be counted on to
reenlist when their terms of service ended.

Reenlistment was being plugged these days with
especial reference to the militia. The act under which
these men had been called into service had been ex-
panded on May 3 by a Presidential proclamation calling
for 42,000 three-year volunteers, to be raised by the
states and mustered into Federal service when complete.
The President had also authorized an increase of 23,000

men in the regular army. His authority to do all of this
was questionable, but it was correctly taken for granted
that Congress would ratify everything when it convened
in July; no one was thinking any longer in terms of
ninety-day war, and so the heat was applied to the
ninety-day soldiers to volunteer en masse for a three-
year term. Some of them responded readily enough, but
a great many of these Pennsylvanians were not in the
least responsive. They might be badly needed, but so far
the government had been unable to outfit them
properly, train them effectively, or even give them any
pay, and now that the troops were within range of the
enemy the Government showed no signs of being able to
use them intelligently. When they put two and two
together, these lads from Pennsylvania were quite
capable of getting four. Their Government had given
them a rush course in disenchantment.

They had done a little moving around. Joe Johnston
had pulled his advance guard out of Harpers Ferry—
which, as later wartime experience was to prove, was
indefensible, a trap for an occupying force rather than a
stronghold—and was concentrating in and around Winchester. By the first of July, Patterson's army had
moved forward and occupied Martinsburg, Harpers
Ferry, and the open country around Charlestown, a few
miles north of Johnston's outposts. John Geyser's regiment, the 7th, appears to have been in camp on the
lower Shenandoah where it could be used in any offensive Patterson cared to order.

Patterson, however, was a bit too confused to go on
the offensive just now. He was ordered to defend the
Potomac River crossings and the line of the railroad to
the west, which involved a defensive posture. He was
also ordered to keep Johnston so busy that no Confederate soldiers could be sent off to Manassas. In addition, he was ordered under no circumstances to risk a
defeat or even a drawn battle, which made it inadvisable
to press Johnston very hard. Besides, Johnston was in-
visible behind a screen of Jeb Stuart's cavalry, so that it
was very hard for even an experienced militia general to

know just where he was or what he was up to. In any case, Patterson realized that the enlistments of most of his soldiers were about to expire and that it was time to begin sending them home.

According to his abilities, Patterson did his best. He edged his troops forward painfully and was in some sort of contact with Confederate skirmishers at about the time when McDowell's troops were approaching Bull Run. Johnston found no difficulty in slipping away from Winchester and taking the railroad cars for Manassas Junction, and a bit later most of Stuart's men followed him. Totally unaware of this, Patterson believed that he had Johnston pinned in place at Winchester, and said that he did not want to force a battle because Johnston had more artillery than he had. (Patterson had been given several batteries, but most of them lacked harness and hence were completely immobilized. Worse yet, Patterson's infantry was in the process of dissolving, and the General reported that "any active operations toward Winchester cannot be thought of until they are replaced by three-year men.") Geyser's regiment got its marching orders on July 21—the day when Beauregard's army, amply reenforced by Johnston, fought and routed McDowell's army at Bull Run. Geyser and his comrades were ordered to march north to Hagerstown, Maryland, where they could take the train for Harrisburg to be mustered out of service.

All of this brought Patterson's career as a soldier to an end, and as his ninety-day warriors left the service, he himself did likewise. Under the circumstances, he would have had to be some sort of miracle worker to do much better than he had actually done, but he left the service under a cloud and nobody was in a mood to listen to any excuses. One of the hard rules of war is that if a general fails, it is really his own fault, no matter how thoroughly the cards had been stacked against him. Patterson saw his name firmly attached to an ignominious failure; the military authorities were glad to see the last of him.

They were also glad to see the last of his troops, whose mood in their final days had turned downright ugly. On July 24 Governor Curtin notified the Secretary of War, Simon Cameron of Pennsylvania—between whom and Curtin there was no love lost—that Harrisburg was brimful of these returned volunteers who were complaining bitterly that they had never been paid, and that this was their chief reason for refusal to reenlist. They added that they lacked camp equipment, so that even when rations were finally issued to them, they were unable to cook them. Curtin considered the situation most serious; his new three-year regiments were beginning to show up, and one of them, ordered to Harpers Ferry, he held back to preserve life and property in Harrisburg until the unhappy ninety-day men could be gotten out of town. To dispose of them it was ordered that each regiment be shipped off to the point nearest the men's homes, where they could be formally mustered out and (it was hoped) paid. For Geyser's regiment this meant Pittsburgh.

The War Department was touched with panic. Secretary Cameron, whose political career might come down in ruins if anything really serious happened in Pennsylvania, did all he could to speed them on their way, wiring to the railway superintendent at Altoona to move those troop trains fast—"There is danger of a terrible riot if this is not done at once." The railroad came through, the terrible riot did not take place and, on July 27, the 7th regiment moved to Pittsburgh, where the matter of final payment and final release was handled with proper dispatch.

A disaster that does not actually take place never gets comprehensive analysis in the post mortems, so this dangerous farce-comedy of the ninety-day men has never come in for very much attention; but it seems clear that a good deal more than the lack of pay was involved here. These, after all, were the cream of the crop of Civil War volunteers, the men who were so powerfully moved by patriotic enthusiasm that they came swarming to enlist within a week of the surrender at

Fort Sumter, and if three months later they had become
so unruly and so determined to get out of the army that
the Secretary of War was afraid of a terrible riot, it is
obvious that something worse than a shortage of ready
cash was bothering them. Part of the trouble apparently
was the extreme looseness—not to say the complete
nonexistence—of military discipline in these hastily
assembled legions. In at least one of the regiments involved, the man who stirred up the soldiers most effectively was their own colonel, and in no regiment did the
company officers have the kind of control that would
have tamped down the mutinous spirit before it took
flame.

Beyond all of this, what would appear to have been
the chief grievance was the men's realization that they
had been wasted. The government that called them to
the colors had not been anywhere nearly ready to use
them; it had not even been ready to clothe them or arm
them or put shoes on their feet; it could feed them only
unsatisfactorily and with great difficulty. In fact, it had
been quite unable to turn them into soldiers, although
they wanted to be soldiers more than they wanted
anything else on earth. The campaign these men were
engaged in was a joke. Making up their brave young
minds to go forth and be tried by fire, these recruits had
found themselves denied the great test of young man-
hood because of the crippling incompetence of the men
who had charge of them. It is no wonder that they
wanted out of this army at the earliest moment.

But they did not feel that they had discharged the
obligation that moved them in the first place. Take John
Geyser as typical. He was paid off and returned to
civilian life at the end of July. He spent a couple of
months looking around, making up his mind about
things—and then, on October 1, 1861, he enlisted for a
three-year hitch in the regular army.

Castle on the Hat

To go from a ninety-day militia unit into the regular army in the summer of 1861 was to cross a gap as wide as anything the American military system could show. The ninety-day lads had enthusiasm (at the start, anyway) and nothing else; the regulars quickly outlived what enthusiasm they ever had, but they had all of the other things the volunteers lacked: hard, impersonal discipline, the equipment a soldier had to have and rigorous schooling in the way to use it, the habit of moving and acting as professionals with professional tradition and leadership rather than as spirited but confused amateurs guided by men of imperfect knowledge. Out of all of this the regular got something to substitute for the volunteer's enthusiasm—pride in being a soldier, a man who had mastered a hard trade and had become a respected journeyman. If the professional lacked the volunteer's capacity for now and then surpassing himself and doing the impossible . . . well, you can't have everything.

The professional's pride ran especially strong in the

Regular Army's Corps of Engineers, which considered
itself the army's elite corps and was commonly accepted
as such by the rest of the army. It was the Corps of
Engineers in which John Geyser enlisted.

The Congressional Act of August 3, 1861, which
enlarged both the regular and the volunteer forces, had
called for a modest increase in the engineer corps. The
corps never was large; at the end of the war, it contained
only eighty-five officers and five companies of enlisted
men. It also contained the United States Military
Academy, from the superintendent down to the lowliest
plebe, but that was a special case; the action part of the
corps consisted of the handful of officers and enlisted
men who traveled with the armies. Three of the engineer
companies were allotted to the Army of the Potomac,
and it was in one of these companies that John Geyser
took his place. With him in Company A, commanded
by Lieutenant C. B. Reese, was his younger brother,
Jacob, who was nineteen and, as a minor, had to
present his father's written consent to his enlistment.

The engineers were the part of the army that was
called on when something needed to be built—roads,
dams, bridges, forts, lines of entrenchments, battery
emplacements, offices and living quarters at headquarters, chapels for religious services, and halls for the
amateur theatricals that were relied on to sustain morale
in the dull winter months. Since the army was forever
needing some of these things, and now and then wanted
a great many of them in a thundering hurry, the engineers were very busy people indeed. Obviously, three
companies could not begin to handle all of these jobs by
themselves, and when any really big project was under-
taken, the engineers got help—whole regiments or even
brigades from the infantry could be and very often were
detailed to stack their arms, take up shovels, and go out
and dig where the engineers told them to.

The point was that it was the engineer officers who
knew where and how things ought to be built: what
spot, for instance, called for an enclosed fort and how
its parapets and dugouts should go and what they ought

to be made of, and how two forts half a mile apart should be connected by entrenchments and how deep and wide and solid these ought to be. The officers would go out with their own men and, with bushels of wooden pegs and many yards of white tape, would have these men mark the lines where digging or other construction ought to take place. Then, if the job was too big, the press-gangs of infantry would get busy, with enlisted engineers as likely as not acting as straw bosses or going on ahead with their own officers to lay out the next job of work. If a bridge over a ravine had been destroyed, the engineers would bring a prefabricated bridge to the scene and put its parts together. If a stream had to be crossed that was too wide for this procedure, it was the engineers who would wheel up the great unwieldy pontoon boats and the bents, stringers, anchors, and so on that accompanied them. They would make a highway bridge that way, standing by to maintain it and to remove it afterward, if necessary, and put it up somewhere else. Inasmuch as enemy skirmishers would interfere with such operations if they could, the engineers had to keep their muskets handy and be ready to use them at any time.

All in all, the engineers were kept very busy, and they got into plenty of fighting as well. It was no place for a man who believed in taking army life as easily as possible. Significantly, the engineers were a high-morale outfit, proving once more a basic fact of military life: that it is idleness and the boredom of hurry-up-and-wait that gets men down, rather than hard work and danger. John Geyser could not possibly have found a military unit where life was in greater contrast to life as he had known it in the 7th Pennsylvania regiment of ninety-day militia.

It was also a unit much less beset by illness. Bloody as the famous Civil War battles were, they took fewer lives than were taken by camp sickness. Especially during the first year of the war, many volunteer regiments were enlisted without any physical examinations whatever— 29 percent of all the volunteer regiments organized in the spring and summer of the first year of the war, according to horrified investigators for the U. S. Sanitary Commission. This, of course, was just asking for trouble because it brought into the army so many thousands of men who simply could not stand the gaff physically. The Commission estimated that, of every ten men lost to the army in 1861, "nine have been needlessly wasted."

Army diet was built around salt pork (either fried to a crisp, or on occasion eaten raw), hardtack, and black coffee. In many units (especially when the army was on the march) this was all there was to eat. Naturally, thousands of men got sick. Many of them suffered from camp diarrhea, and although this could usually be cured by a return to decent food, there were many cases of amoebic dysentery, which often could not be cured at all. And if men ate better in camp than when on the road, in other respects camp life was worse. Wall tents or makeshift huts with canvas roofs were poorly sited, without flooring, bunks consisting usually of dead leaves or straw heaped behind low board partitions on the ground. The places were usually subject to flooding after every rain, and all in all, were not much better than pigsties. Pneumonia was common; reading about those living quarters makes one wonder how any soldier avoided it.

To be sure, this did not go on forever—certainly not after Joe Hooker took command of the Army of the Potomac in the winter of 1863. In the course of time, things got better organized, and the worst evils were remedied. But the fact remains that taking the war as a whole, a man risked his life simply by being in the army, even if he never got near a battlefield.

From much of this, however, the Regulars were exempt. Doctors may have had limited knowledge, but they were not stupid. They had fairly good ideas about the way to lay out a camp so that the soldiers could at least be dry and clean, and the West Pointers who commanded platoons and companies would see to it that proper rules were laid down and followed. The Sanitary

Commission that found so many things wrong in the Volunteer Army remarked pointedly that these criticisms did not apply to the Regulars, "with their experience of camp police, discipline, subordination and the sanitary conditions of military life." If this was true of Regulars generally, it was especially true of the engineers, who were builders. (Their huts would most likely have floors.)

So the Geyser brothers got into the Regular Engineers, and John seems to have thought about the kind of war he was going to fight. In his job at the Allegheny City machine shop he had been a patternmaker—a job for a man of skills, which won him a rating as artificer in the Corps of Engineers. He had also studied drawing, which fitted in with his job as patternmaker. Around the beginning of the year 1862, he made some sort of deal with the proprietors of the New York *Illustrated News* to do army sketches for them.

Apparently John Geyser was a little too honest. He made sketches and they were good ones, but they did not quite hit what the New York editors considered the popular taste. The sketches were too thoughtful, too quiet, too undramatic . . . like all editors, these gentlemen believed that they knew just what their readers wanted. (All editors believe that, of course, and if you ever become an editor, you will believe it, too, but there is one thing to remember: if your belief happens to be right you are a great editor. But if it is wrong, you are nobody at all, and pretty soon you will be in another line of work. John Geyser seems to have sent his sketches to a board of nobodies.) What young Geyser did was write his personal memoirs in the form of penciled illustrations—a campfire scene here, soldiers loafing by a creekside grove there, a soldier's face reflecting the bleak wisdom that comes to a young man who signs up for Heaven-knows-what because strange impulses jar youth's desires out of gear—and this was not in the least what the Board of Nobodies wanted. They wanted picturesque ranks of dauntless youths marching into Battle and dying bloodlessly by the numbers. Although Geyser

saw a God's plenty of young men being killed in battle,
he apparently saw nothing that would fit the picture-
book accounts, and so he did not draw it that way. In
the end, none of his sketches were printed, but he kept
the sketchbook, and its pictures are presented here. He
followed the truth as he saw it, which is more than a
good many editors can ever say.

He put in most of the fall and early winter learning
the elements of his new trade. The new engineers went
to Washington for their training and were housed in
buildings next to the arsenal on the point of ground just
southward where the East Branch joins the main tide
of the Potomac. Quarters were somewhat spartan, although compared with what the Pennsylvania militia
regiment had given John Geyser, this must have seemed
like living in the White House. The rooms were
crowded, and for a time, there were no cots or bed rolls
and the recruits had to sleep on the floor in their overcoats. In the volunteer army, new soldiers would have
complained bitterly about this, but these lads took it in
their stride because the men in charge of them kept them
busy and did not encourage critical comments by enlisted men. There were veterans around who could
answer a recruit's questions without making him feel
stupid for having asked, and above all, there were the
old regular army noncoms who could take the clumsy
newcomer down to the waterside and show him what to
do with the great ungainly pontoon boats that were
awaiting attention there. Some of these noncoms were
legendary characters. Most noteworthy probably was
Sergeant Fred Gerber, who apparently had been everywhere and done everything. It was whispered that he
had even studied for the priesthood until he and his
superiors realized that Holy Orders were not for him.
He had been in Mexico and on the western plains, he
was an expert at just about everything—"Quartermaster and drill master, butcher and blacksmith, rigger
and boatsman," as an admiring ex-pupil recorded. He
had vast pride in his calling, and he argued firmly that it
was much more of an honor to be ranking noncom in a

company of engineers than to be a commissioned officer in any other outfit.

In this he was vigorously upheld by Captain James C. Duane, who commanded the engineer battalion in the Army of the Potomac. Duane understood that a high-morale outfit is composed of men who considered themselves better than other soldiers, and he understood also that if they believe this strongly enough, they begin to behave accordingly, so that pretty soon they are better. He discouraged his noncoms who were offered commissions in volunteer infantry regiments. To one such he said, "Why, President Lincoln can make a brigadier general in five minutes, but it has taken five years to make you an engineer soldier." The men of Company A took enormous pride in the engineer corps insignia, a metal replica of an armory with battlemented towers, worn on the front of the hat along with a letter designating the man's company. Early in 1862, it was proudly recorded, the castle and letter would pass a man "anywhere around Washington." Captain Duane stimulated this pride, and when the army raised and used a couple of volunteer engineer regiments and the castle insignia were seen everywhere, Duane sternly ordered the regulars not to wear theirs at all. (If mere volunteers could wear them, they were no longer badges of distinction. Clearly, Captain Duane was a hard case.) It was more than a year before the regulars got their castles back.

Meanwhile, there was a rigorous training to go through. Sergeant Gerber took the lads down to the waterfront one day to introduce them to pontoon boats, and when the budding engineers saw them, they were moved to laughter at the idea that these things could actually be lugged across country and used to make bridges. Sergeant Gerber buckled down to it, and they buckled down with him, and the laughter died away for good. The men learned to move the scows and they learned to build bridges with them, and under the doughty sergeant, they did it all "by the numbers"; it was not only necessary to fix a floating path so that the

army could cross a stream, but it was also necessary to
do it in style, with a snap.

The recruits saw other things, too. There were two
dozen big weapons to carry the pontoon boats, and
horses to pull them; there were ten other wagons full of
the various specialized tools the engineers had to be
always ready to use—in December the artificers went to
the river to repair the bow of the steamer *Henry
Jenkins*, which had been shot up by Confederate batteries on the lower Potomac—and there were other
wagons loaded with picks and shovels for use in building fortifications. The recruits had to learn about all of
these things at once, because General McClellan, commander of the Army of the Potomac, was about ready
to move on Richmond.

As part of his preparation for this advance, Mc-
Clellan wanted to post a strong detachment in the lower
Shenandoah Valley at Winchester, to protect the army's
right flank and rear while it went adventuring along the
James River. General Nathaniel P. Banks was appointed to command this force, and his supply line
would run northeast twenty-odd miles from Winchester
to Harpers Ferry. The bridge over the Potomac at Harpers Ferry had been burned, and its sooty stone piers
stood desolate in the middle of the river; to build an entirely new bridge there would take altogether too much
time, so the engineers were called on to lay a pontoon
bridge. This was an intricate operation, made especially
so in February of 1862 by the fact that heavy rains in the
mountains had swollen the river so that its surface was
many feet above the normal level, and its current had a
twisting, unruly strength. Company A of the engineers'
battalion was sent to the scene to do the job.

Usually the engineers worked in obscurity, and about
all we ever hear about them is that they came in, did a
job, and then went away. But this time, which happened
to be the first time the Geyser brothers got in on a major
task, a volunteer infantryman on the bank of the river
was watching attentively and he made notes. To quote
from his account:

"As early as nine o'clock about one hundred men came down opposite the Ferry, just above the old bridge, and broke into little groups, in military precision. Four or five with spades and other implements improvised a wooden abutment on the shore; another party rowed against the stream, moored a scow, and let it drift down until it was opposite the wooden abutments; then a party of ten advanced, each two men carrying a claw-balk, or timbers fitted with a claw, one of which held the gunwale of the boat, the other the shore abutment. Twenty men now came down on the left with planks, one inch thick, six inches wide and fifteen feet long, narrowed at each end; these they laid across the five joists or balks, and returned on the right. Another party meanwhile moored another boat, which dropped downstream opposite the one already bridged; five joists, each twenty feet along, were laid upon the gunwales by five men; these were fastened by those in the boat by means of ropes to cleats or hooks provided for that purpose on the side of the scow, which was shoved off from the shore until the shore end of the balk rested upon the shore boat. These were covered with planks in the same manner as before; side-rails of joists were lashed down with ropes to secure the whole.

"So one after another of the boats was dropped into position until a bridge several hundred feet long reached from the Maryland to the Virginia shore, for the passage of artillery and every description of munitions for an army. Owing to the force of the current a large rope-cable was stretched from shore to shore fifty feet above the bridge, and the upper end of each boat was stayed to the cable by a smaller rope. The rushing current bent the bridge into a half-moon curve. The clock-like precision with which these men worked showed them to be the drilled engineers and pontoniers of the regular army."

So the bridge was finished, and the first man on it was General McClellan himself, who came out to congratulate the engineers, officers and men, for having done a hard job expeditiously. (It was not just by accident that McClellan was greatly admired by the rank

and file of this army.) General Banks occupied Winchester, and now he had a supply line.

The Potomac, however, was a nuisance; the pontoon
bridge held that crescent-shaped curve, the river surged
up now and then in unexpected rises, and it seemed
quite possible that pontoon boats, balks, plans, and all,
might break up and go downstream when the spring
floods came on, in which case General Banks would be
in a very bad fix. At best, these pontoon bridges were
touchy; troops marching across them were not allowed
to march in step but had to go "route step," because the
rhythmic left-right-left-right of a marching column was
likely to set up a swaying motion that would make the
bridge collapse. Also, officers, couriers, cavalrymen or
other mounted persons were not allowed to trot their
horses on these bridges, for the same reason. General
McClellan ordered a more substantial bridge to be laid.

For this bridge, they would use canal boats—heavy,
blunt-ended craft, seventy or eighty feet long and fourteen feet wide, drawing no more than two feet of water
when unloaded; these were to be floated up the Chesapeake and Ohio Canal to a point opposite Harpers
Ferry, where there was a lift-lock feeding into the
Potomac River. Put into the river via that lock, these
ponderous craft could make a bridge that would give
General Banks a good supply line no matter how the
Potomac misbehaved.

Alas for pious hopes! Somebody had figured things
wrong—or more likely forgotten to figure them at all.
The expedition set off up the canal from Washington,
got to the lift-lock opposite Harpers Ferry, where the
boats were to be put into the Potomac—and at this
moment it was found that the boats were just five inches
too wide to go through the locks.

This drew from President Lincoln (who was beginning to have his doubts about General McClellan
anyway) one of the most outspoken displays of bad tem-
per ever recorded of that ordinarily soft-spoken and
tolerant magistrate. McClellan sent his chief of staff,
General R. B. Marcy, off to the White House to explain

what had happened, and the General stood right in the line of fire.

"Why in the nation, General Marcy," said Lincoln, "couldn't the General have known whether a boat would go through that lock before spending a million dollars getting them there? . . . It seems to me that if I wished to know whether a boat would go through a hole, or a lock, common sense would teach me to go and measure it." Around Washington that winter the accepted wisecrack was that this expedition had died of lockjaw.

In the end, of course, the canal boats were sent down to Washington, and the engineers finally built a bridge on the stone piers of the one that had been burned, and General Banks got along very nicely until Stonewall Jackson came up in mid-spring and knocked him loose from his supply line at the southern end.

The Peninsula

From Harpers Ferry the engineers returned to Washington, and early spring found them working on the city's fortifications. They were in Virginia now, with Geyser's company, mostly in and around Fairfax, and they were part of McClellan's effort to build such a massive chain of defensive works that no matter what happened the Confederacy could not break into the capital city. The line of works north of the Potomac had largely been finished, and that part of the job was not so pressing anyway. Now the job was to build a shield all the way from Alexandria on the Potomac south of Washington to the Chain Bridge opposite Georgetown. Counting the forts in Maryland, the engineers altogether laid out and built thirty-three miles of defensive works.

These were cunningly devised. There was no attempt to make a continuous line of entrenchments, but the effect was about the same. From Fort Ethan Allan, covering the approach to the Chain Bridge, to Forts Ellsworth and Lyon guarding Alexandria, there was an intricate network of strong points with names then important but long since forgotten—Forts DeKalb, Bennett, Corcoran, Woodbury, Cass, Tillinghast, and all the rest—each crowning a hill or a gentle rise in the ground so that anyone who attacked would have to fight uphill, while artillery behind heavy embankments reached far out to strike the attacker's guns and the infantry forming for the assault. Each fort could also be covered by cannon fire from at least two others, one to the right and one to the left. Where roads led into these gaps, obstacles had been prepared—felled trees with interlocked sharpened branches pointing south, or ponderous logs studded with pointed stakes, ready to be planted in the open spaces at the first alarm. The invader might cut these to bits with axes or shove them bodily out of the way, but this would take time, and the obstacles were all sited so that the men who tried to remove them would be under artillery and rifle fire while they worked. When the whole layout was finished, McClellan (who was himself an engineer, originally) estimated that with a garrison of 34,000 men and with forty field guns to supplement the guns already emplaced, the Washington lines could be held against any conceivable assault and would be invulnerable even to formal siege procedures.

The engineers had a good deal of help doing all of this. Not only were regiments and brigades detailed for pick-and-shovel work, but a great many civilian laborers from the Washington area were hired to help, so that by the middle of March or thereabouts, the defenses were complete. It was time to start for Richmond, and on March 17 the first contingents embarked. They used every imaginable kind of water craft—ocean steamers, river steamers, schooners, barges nudged along by tugboats, all going down the Potomac for Chesapeake Bay and Old Point Comfort, heading for the lower tip of the great Virginia peninsula between the James and York rivers—a flat land of good farms, innumerable water courses, second-growth timber, stately tidewater mansions, and a few villages. The Federal

high command did not know nearly as much as it
thought it knew about this area, though, and one of the
things it did not know was that this flat low country was
subject to floods whenever heavy rains touched the
rivers. This was a matter which the corps of engineers
would eventually find of particular interest.

That, of course, came later. For the engineers the first
step was to get down to the tip of the Virginia peninsula
in the general vicinity of Fort Monroe and make it
possible for the invading army to get its soldiers and its
endless chain of wagons, guns, munitions, food stuffs,
and general odds and ends safely off of the transports
and onto dry land in proper order. Unfortunately, except at Fort Monroe itself, wharves were lacking, no one
having imagined that it would some day be necessary to
put ashore here an army of 120,000 men. The engineers,
assisted by the Quartermaster Corps, were the lads to
provide the wharves.

They began by assembling canal boats. (These did not
have to go through any skimpy locks, so the precise
measurements, gunwale to gunwale, did not matter
much.) Down from the upper reaches of the Chesapeake
came whole fleets of these heavy, snub-nosed craft,
which ran from sixty to seventy feet in length and were
uniformly fourteen feet wide. Take two of these, ar-
range them twelve feet apart, bind them firmly to each
other with heavy cross timbers, and then build a solid
plank deck over the top, and you would get a floating
platform forty feet wide and forty-five or fifty feet long:
a whole battery of field artillery (six guns, with their
limbers) could be taken from the transports and put on
this device, and their horses could be accommodated on
a similar one, and then a tugboat could nuzzle the two
rafts as close to shore as possible. At that moment, with
the rafts securely anchored, the engineers could build
bridges, with pontoons or with prefabricated timbers,
leading to dry land, and the guns and horses could be
taken ashore. Once this was done, you had a perfectly
serviceable wharf, a T-shaped affair with a thick
crossbar and a stubby vertical member, and a transport

could easily moor alongside and discharge its cargo. It was also possible to fasten two pontoons together side by side, with flooring over the top, and make a diminutive barge that would carry one field piece. Since the barge would float in nine inches of water it was simple to warp it close to the beach and use ropes and human muscles to haul the gun ashore.

The pontoons were also useful as landing craft. One pontoon could carry forty men, plus a crew of three, and troops could go ashore without requiring the transports to come within a hundred yards of the beach. It turned out that the ships' masters were not used to this sort of thing and distrusted it mightily, while the soldiers, most of whom had never so much as smelled salt water before, distrusted it a great deal more, and things went very slowly. When the pontoons were brought alongside the transports, the soldiers went down the rope ladders cautiously, one at a time, each man waiting until the man ahead of him had got off before starting down himself. So it took half a day to unload a few hundred men, and with more than 100,000 men to disembark, it began to look as if the war would die of inaction before the army got ashore.

As usual, the engineers knew what to do. They devised and built inclined ramps so that the men could simply walk down from the decks to the scows; presently 2,000 men were being landed in one hour, and in no time this was stepped up to 8,000 men in three hours. Before long, McClellan had his army on firm ground, ready to go. By the end of April he could start for Richmond, moving up the peninsula between the York and the James rivers.

As the army took to the roads, the three companies of engineers learned that they were going to have help. The War Department had enlisted a brigade of volunteer engineers whose right to the castle badge irritated Captain Duane so much. There were two regiments, the 15th and 50th New York, under the overall command of Brigadier General Daniel Woodbury. The regular engineers were not folded into this organization, but remained

separate, responsible directly to army headquarters,
moving with the headquarters people and subtly ranked
as superior to these volunteers. As a matter of fact, the
volunteer army was teeming with men quite capable of
playing the part of military engineers if some capable
officer directed them. Troops from cities and towns
were full of mechanics of high and low degree. Regiments from Maine, Pennsylvania, Michigan, and Wis-
consin contained hundreds of men from the lumber
camps who knew all anyone will ever know about the
way to use saws and axes. Frontier troops had men who
could cut roads through the wilderness, improvise
bridges, and build cabins and sheds out of anything that
came to hand.

It developed that the typical American was a jack-of-
all-trades. General U. S. Grant found this out a year
later in the Vicksburg campaign when his troops built a
thirty-mile military road through the swamps, including
two three-hundred-foot floating bridges which, as a
regular engineer officer admiringly pointed out, "were
built by green volunteers who had never seen a bridge
train nor had an hour's drill or instruction in bridge
building." Grant himself praised the volunteers'
abilities by saying that "there is nothing which men are
called upon to do, mechanical or professional, that accomplished adepts cannot be found for the duty
required in almost every regiment." This may have been
more noticeable in the western armies. Most of the
regular engineer troops were in the East, and the
Westerners relied more on the green volunteers simply
because they had to.

In any case, the whole peninsular campaign was a
time of uninterrupted toil for the engineers—making
roads, draining swamps, putting up bridges, building
fortifications—and if they got a good deal of help from
the infantry, there were one or two unusual features involved. Some infantry companies detailed for these jobs
performed well, and some were just about useless: a by-
product of that all but ineradicable shortcoming of so
many Civil War regiments—lack of discipline and

military knowledge on the part of the company officers. In far too many cases the officers of a detailed company simply turned their men over to the nearest engineer officer and then took it for granted that they had done all they were supposed to do; so they retired to a pleasant spot in the shade (or if there was no shade, the nearest spot where the clanking and shuffling and swearing of sweating construction workers would not be a disturbance) and stretched out to smoke and loaf and take their ease until quitting time. With their officers behaving so, the enlisted men naturally did as little as possible, and there was not much the engineers could do about it.

It was also noticed that there was a steady depletion of the tools the infantry men used, especially of the axes. When a regiment was in what looked like a permanent camp—which is to say when it seemed likely to stay in the same spot for at least a week—the men would take pains to make themselves comfortable, and an ax was an extremely useful thing to have. (With an ax you could cut up firewood, or chop off leafy branches to shade a tent, or reduce saplings to the proper size and length for tent floorings; altogether, an ax was to be prized.) So detailed men developed the habit of taking their axes back to camp with them and forgetting to return them. When the army moved, as it was forever doing, most of the axes were simply abandoned. An ax is a heavy, unhandy thing for an overloaded foot soldier to carry, so hardly any men bothered to carry them when they went over the camp grounds and battlefield after the campaign ended, and possibly a lot of axes were simply lost in the underbrush and the mud. If their component parts have not rotted or rusted away altogether, they are very likely there to this day.

When the army moved as far as Yorktown, the bright climactic town of the revolutionary epic, it had to come to a halt. The Confederates were solidly entrenched. There were streams and ponds where the Federals had not expected anything of the kind; in effect, the defense works ran all the way from the York to the James; there

was no way to go around them and taking them by
storm seemed impossible, because there was a great deal
of Rebel artillery mounted in secure forts. McClellan
surveyed the situation and concluded (rightly or
wrongly) that the only thing to do was to bring up his
own siege guns and blast the defensive works out of the
way. This put it up to the engineers, because the roads
by which those ponderous weapons had to move did not
exist, and because when the weighty guns and mortars
were at last advanced, they would have to be put into
prepared fortifications so that the Confederates could
not take them under destructive fire before they were
ready to be used.

The way to prepare the emplacements, build the
roads, get the artillery train off the boats and onto the
roads, and move the ungainly, oversized, cantankerous
masses of iron and steel to the places where they could
at last open fire without subjecting their own gun crew
to destruction—all of this was in the book. The
engineers knew the book by heart, and once the job was
well under way, the end was inevitable. It was routine,
as a matter of fact, and it would hardly be worth men-
tioning except that it involved such an enormous
amount of hard, inglorious, thankless work.

Napoleon remarked that an army goes forward on its
stomach, and it is the heart-stuff of cherished legend
that battles are won by human valor; but there is
something to be said for the idea that a most important
factor is simply human muscle—the will-to-work of
tired, over-taxed, sometimes discouraged young men
who shoulder an army on toward victory simply by
digging in their toes and shoving. At times, of course,
all of the hard work is wasted because the high command does not know what to do with what has been
gained by the hard work, in which case the workers can
do no better than turn a new page and start all over
again. Anyway, when McClellan made up his mind to
blow the Rebel army out of its Yorktown lines with his
siege train, he served notice that 101 pieces of heavy
ordnance would have to be brought ashore and posted

where it could begin crunching the Confederates.

Of these 101 pieces, slightly more than half were no more than slightly enlarged models of ordinary field artillery—4½-inch Rodman rifles, 30-pound Parrott rifles, a few eight-inch howitzers, a number of eight-inch mortars, and a handful of long-range breech-loading Whitworths from England. These were hard to handle, and they could not take the field with the ordinary artillery battalions, but getting them from here to there was no great problem on a moderately decent road. It was the others that caused the trouble.

These were the rock-crushers—eleven 100-pound Parrotts, two 200-pounders, ten 13-inch sea-coast mortars and twenty-five 10-inch mortars. If they were to move any distance, it had to be by rail or by water; the lightest of them weighed four and one half tons and the biggest weighed twice that much, and in a land of totally unpaved roads, subject to frequent rains that turned the whole countryside into mud, they were altogether unmanageable. Fortunately, at Yorktown there was a stream that led in from the outer rivers to the heart of the area where McClellan wanted to set up his batteries. One at a time, the unwieldy pieces were floated ashore while the engineers made things ready for them.

Moving these Goliaths after they were put ashore was the real problem. The monsters did not pretend to be wheeled vehicles. They had to be carried—on flat sledges, usually, inching along laboriously on rollers, with extra logs carried along to make tripod cranes when it came time to unload. With stout ropes, pulleys, and plenty of manpower, the big cannons were taken from their original carriages and carried on sling cars, monstrous affairs with grotesquely oversized wheels. It went very slowly, of course, and often enough a whole regiment stacked arms and took hold of the drag lines. It was an army engineer, incidentally, who said after his Civil War experience that he no longer wondered how the Egyptians moved the immense rocks that built the pyramids; put enough men on a rope, he had found, and you could move anything.

Much of the toil of actually moving the siege train
devolved on the army's artillerists. It was the engineers
who had to build the roads, making them wide and solid
and as smooth as possible, and then had to make things
ready for the guns and mortars on the firing line. The
gunners reassembled the pieces and stood by to use them
when word came to commence firing.

Making things ready involved building an extended
chain of fortifications. For the big mortars this was
fairly simple, although it did call for the digging of a
great amount of dirt. The flight of a mortar shell was
like a pop fly to centerfield, a high-arching curve that
could take the shell over hills and trees and walls and
drop it in an enemy gun emplacement. Fixing positions
for these weapons therefore simply meant gouging out
the sheltered side of a hill, and while this did call for
much digging, it was simple enough once the banks were
properly revetted, so they would not slide down in muddy ruin after every rain. The cannon themselves needed
actual walls, with firing places arranged so that the guns
could either fire over the embankment or through open
embrasures.

Whether they were going to revet earthen banks or
build substantial ramparts, the engineers needed a great
deal of material they themselves had to prepare in advance. Before the Yorktown lines could be built, it was
necessary for the Geysers and their comrades to spend
many days making fascines and gabions, and if they had
never heard of these before, they were to hear a great
deal about them from then on.

Fascines were long bundles of brush or stakes tightly
bound together and useful in various ways. Place them
against the bank of a cut-away hillside or along the sides
of a trench and you had proper revetments. They were
also useful for emergency roadwork, to fill in a ditch or
patch up a hollow place in a country road. In a pinch,
they could be strung out along the ground, covered with
dirt and made to form low breast works.

Gabions were more complicated. They were woven of
stout withes, or the roots of trees, or sometimes out of

limber strips of metal, to make hollow cylindrical
baskets without tops or bottoms, two or three feet in
diameter and perhaps four feet tall. Stood on end, close
together, filled with earth and then crowned and reinforced with sandbags, they made a fairly substantial
rampart, able to protect gunners against a moderate
amount of artillery fire. During the first weeks at
Yorktown, the engineers made hundreds of gabions and
taught detailed infantry men how to make other hundreds of them; and at last, yard by yard, McClellan had
his siege guns in place and it was time to blast the Rebels
out of there and take off for Richmond.

The job had taken just a month, and army headquarters prepared to open the great bombardment on May 4,
1862. But the Confederates, of course, had known what
was going on, and they realized perfectly well that when
McClellan's siege train opened up the Confederate lines
would be destroyed. The existence of those lines had imposed on the invader a month's delay, which was as
much as Richmond could hope for and more than it had
dared to expect. Consequently, on the night of May 3,
the Confederates slipped out of their lines and went up
the peninsula in retreat. When the Yankee gunners got
ready to open fire, they found that they had nothing to
shoot at.

McClellan consoled himself with the thought that the
wear and tear of a battle had, after all, not been
necessary, and any of his foot soldiers who had been in
action before undoubtedly felt the same consolation. It
is just as likely that the engineers themselves had a
feeling of anticlimax. All of that work and no shooting!

Dress Parade
Every Evening

Moving cautiously, as if it could not quite believe that things were as good as they seemed, the Army of the Potomac set out after the retreating Confederates on May 5. It caught up with them at Williamsburg, where the Southerners were waiting behind good entrenchments, and a murderous fire-fight developed in which each side lost some two thousand men and proved nothing except that nobody was going to give up one acre of Southern real estate without demanding payment in full, in advance. While the payments were being made, the engineers assembled themselves near Yorktown, got the siege train out of the forts and back on the transports, loaded the infernally awkward pontoons on wagons for overland movement, and camped (as the battalion historian proudly recorded) on the field where Cornwallis had surrendered. Then they marched through Yorktown, following the army, camping at night without tents or cooked food, and by May 13 they

found themselves up in front once more, clearing the
road for the fighting men.

As usual, this meant hard work. To begin with, the
Rebels had felled many trees and these lay across the imperfect road, to be cut up and dragged away by the
engineers and destroyed in great bonfires that raised
pillars of smoke by day and pillars of fire by night. The
pontoon train, of course, was hauled along, and it was
forever getting stuck in the heavy mud, from which it
had to be extricated by hand. Most of the time the road
had to be corduroyed, which meant that an infinite
number of small trees had to be cut up into eight-foot
lengths that were laid side by side in the mud and bound
down by longer timbers fastened along the outer ends.
Once corduroyed, a road could be traversed by wagons,
guns, and what-not. By general agreement, the road was
the bumpiest and generally the most uncomfortable
highway yet devised by mortal man. Still, it could be
used . . . unless a sudden flood floated the logs away, in
which case it was start all over again and don't bother to
swear about it, because you are going to need your wind
for work.

Someone had misinformed General McClellan about
the roads on the Virginia peninsula. Around the first of
the year, when he was selling his idea for a move up the
peninsula in top-level conferences at Washington, the
General had said that the country was flat and the soil
was sandy, so that an army of invasion could use the
roads without any trouble. In a way this was true; the
country was indeed flat, and the roads were good
enough, as long as the weather remained dry. When the
rains came, however, matters were different.

Richmond lay on the left bank of the James, and the
peninsula clearly offered a straight path to its front
door. The one unfortunate factor was the presence of
the Chickahominy River, a most unimportant little river
that rose somewhere in the empty country to the
northwest, came down the peninsula between the York
and the James, and entered the James some twenty or

thirty miles below the Confederate capital. The Chickahominy was no more than thirty feet wide, and in most
places a man could wade across it without getting wet
above his belt buckle. It had low banks, coming down
through a flat bottom land overgrown with thickets and
scrubby little trees, and several hundred yards away
from these characterless banks there were low bluffs,
rising steeply but not really very high. It did not seem to
be an obstacle that had to be taken seriously.

The trouble was that in warm weather the Virginia
rains were frequent and often torrential, and McClellan
ruefully noted that, as a result, the Chickahominy was
"subject to frequent, sudden and great variations in the
volume of water, and a rise of a few feet overflowed the
bottom lands on both sides." When this happened, as it
very often did in the spring of 1862, the Chickahominy
could not be forded anywhere, and the approaches on
each side led through hopeless swamps, with three feet
of water over mud. The engineers came up when the
river was on its good behavior and they built bridges
with pontoons, sometimes, and also with planks and
saplings laid on log-and-dirt cribs placed on the banks.
After a short time the Chickahominy was flooded and
all of these bridges were washed out. The engineers
brought up more material and tried again, and this time
they had to build long causeways across the swamps to
bring roads from dry land down to the banks of the
rivers. Often enough the men had to work waist-deep in
water to build these causeways, and to complicate matters, the Rebels perched in trees on their side of the river
and took potshots at them.

The engineers usually had to provide their own
protection. When a detachment was sent forward to
work, half of the men would take their muskets, plow
ahead through the water, and try to keep the Confederate riflemen in check while the other half built the
bridge and did what they could do to provide it with
usable approaches.

Bringing the pontoon trains forward was a constant
trial. The wagons that carried these scows were about

the most ungainly and generally obstreperous wheeled vehicles ever put on a roadway, and the roads by which they had to move up were always muddy and usually under a foot or two of water. The wagons bogged down often enough, in which cases the engineers had to boost them out of the mud by hand, and now and then an underwater causeway of logs, fascines, stray rocks, and anything else that was handy had to be built. Sometimes this took place under enemy fire. After a few days of this grueling labor, the men were dead on their feet, and a pause in the march even for a moment saw all hands flop down and go sound asleep—provided, of course, that the surrounding terrain was not under water. They slept thus when they came out of the swamps near an army camp at Cumberland. A volunteer general leading his brigade by happened to see them, was scandalized, and put the whole battalion under arrest. (This was rectified as soon as word got to army headquarters.)

Most of McClellan's army remained on the left bank of the river, in communication with the great army base at White House, on the York River, but two corps had crossed the Chickahominy to maintain contact with the Confederates. At the end of May the heavy rains came, all but one of the bridges over the river were washed out, and General Joseph E. Johnston, the Confederate commander, seeing a chance to destroy a large fraction of the invading army while it was isolated, ordered his troops to attack in a two-day battle known variously as Fair Oaks and Seven Pines.

The attack came at a bad time for the Federals. For a few hours Johnston had the isolated Union troops at his mercy. He might have totally destroyed them except that some of his commanders got mixed up on their assignments so that the full force of the Confederate assault was not delivered. These shortcomings could be remedied, however, and the Union army faced sheer catastrophe—except for that one remaining bridge, a rickety, crib-and-stringer affair with foaming water over its floor boards and the whole structure looking as if it would be swept downstream at any moment.

McClellan ordered the powerful Second Corps to go
across at all hazards. Commander of this corps was
General Edwin V. Sumner, a rough-cast old diehard
who is accurately characterized by his nickname, "Bull
of the Woods." He had been an army officer since
before McClellan was born, and although he had many
limitations—he was old, and totally lacking in im-
agination—he had the old army notion that orders
from the Commanding General were to be obeyed no
matter what. He had a booming voice that could knock
the sky loose, and nothing in this world or the next ever
scared him. Sumner brought the head of his column
down to the river and found the swaying bridge
precariously held in position by ropes running from
midstream to the bank. He was warned that the bridge
was highly unsafe and must not be used. Sumner snor-
ted at this, expressing his reaction simply: "I am *ordered!*" and he took his corps out on the bridge.

Startled engineers who looked on reported that
nothing but the weight of the moving column kept the
bridge in place. Nobody ever quite understood how it
was done, but somehow the bridge stayed put and the
Second Corps got across and went into action in time to
save the besieged corps from destruction. It was remarked that of the corps artillery only one gun could be
got up front; the roads were too muddy and too much
under water, and getting that one gun there was as much
as this army corps could manage.

Anyway, even if this disaster had been averted, a new
one might easily occur, for the bridge broke up and
floated away as soon as the last soldiers got across, and
the army was still divided with what looked like an im-
passable flood rampaging between its two halves. It was
of the first importance to rebuild some bridges, and
there was no sleep for any engineers this night.

It was not a good time for working on bridges. The
night was blacker than Exodus midnight in Egypt, there
was a strangling rain that made all of the earlier rains
look mild, the river kept rising, sweeping far over its
banks and moving swiftly enough to carry a worker off

his feet. Even Duane finaly admitted it was too much and had his engineers huddle where they could to wait uncomfortably for morning, soaking wet, totally unsheltered, and as hungry as they were weary. The volunteer engineer brigade, trying to rebuild bridges farther upstream, got along no better. The prefabricated bents, stringers, railings, and flooring which they had stacked on the bank went floating away on the surging waters and were never seen again. On this night, nobody built anything.

With morning, the several jobs were resumed, and eventually all bridges were replaced. Full communication was restored, although the job was a continuing headache. The approaches to the bridges, especially on the Confederate side, consisted of extended causeways—corduroyed roads, mostly, raised above ordinary ground level on earth packed between logs—and long stretches of these causeways were under water; working on them so that guns and wagons could use them was hard, especially because some sections were under fire by Southern riflemen. Now and then Duane's engineers had to send their own riflemen two hundred yards in advance to clear the way, and there were casualties. McClellan's exasperation is reflected in the language of his report, which complained that "the whole face of the country is a perfect bog, with men working up to their waists in water." An engineer battalion historian remarked glumly that the work "became very trying; the water had fallen, dead animals and filth were encountered; heavy showers at night rendered a dry sleep impossible, and the health of the command suffered."

This is not an account of the ins and outs of the seven-days Battle for Richmond. It is simply a glimpse at the part played in that struggle by the regular battalion of engineers who shared in the dangers, got more than a full share of the hard work and discomfort, and won so little glory that even a fairly well-posted student of the Civil War usually remembers nothing about them except that they built bridges.

They built bridges indeed, under conditions ranging
from the merely difficult to the downright impossible.
(There was a nine-hundred-foot job built just west of
the mouth of a tributary known as Boatswain's Swamp,
where the engineers had to work in water that was over
their heads; this project took six days.) They also built
small forts to protect the bridgeheads, and they went
farther from the river to build redoubts and earthworks
and great frowning gun emplacements for the front-line
infantry, a line six miles long, measured foot by foot in
sweat. On most nights they had to repair the bridgehead
forts which the Rebels had bombarded from batteries
on the higher ground to the west and south. Along with
everything else, they built a hospital for their own sick
and wounded men, by a nice little spring that bubbled
up at the edge of woods at a place where the ground was
dry.

Having done all of this, and having lost much sleep
and sweat in the doing, the engineers now were ordered
to destroy everything and get set to go through the same
process somewhere else. The battle was going against
McClellan and he had to bring all of his army and its
equipment over to the right bank of the Chickahominy
and make his way to a secure camp on the James River.

So the bridges that had been built with so much care
had to be dismantled, and because the army's position
was changing so fast, the dismantling had to be done at
substantial risk, sometimes under fire, sometimes with
armed enemies coming down along the banks ready to
capture bridges, engineers and all, if there was any lost
motion. One group sent to dismantle New Bridge, far-
thest upstream, had to work especially fast, and the men
were under orders to use their axes as weapons if attacked. They finished the job and moved to higher
ground only to find themselves between the lines of the
Union and Confederate troops that were just beginning
the bloody battle of Gaines' Mill. Somehow, they got
out alive. One bridge had to be destroyed by men working under a steady fire. Another party at another bridge

had to put down tools, pick up rifles and beat off a
cavalry attack before finishing its task. When the army
got away from the Chickahominy, its entire wagon train
had to go along the roadway the engineers had made
across White Oak swamp, and they trundled along
through a hot steamy night, where marching infantry
had discarded blankets by the hundred. One soggy
hollow in the road the engineers actually repaired by pil-
ing in brush, covering this with discarded blankets and
putting earth on top. It worked, and one teamster said
that it was like taking his wagon along a rubber carpet.

One way or another, the army got through and plod-
ded down to its refuge in a sprawling camp at Harrison's Landing on the James River, where the navy
waited with powerful warships to keep the enemy from
getting in too close, and where the engineers made
roads, built bridges, and laid out a set of protective field
works. While the bulk of the army got safely behind
these works, the engineers returned to the high plateau
of Malvern Hill, where the rear guard was dug in behind
a great rank of field artillery to keep the pursuing Confederates from getting in close and turning the refuge
into a death trap. The pursuing Confederates tried hard
enough, unwisely but valiantly, and in some lapse of
skill, Robert E. Lee ordered a direct assault on an invulnerable front and lost five or six thousand men. The
engineers found themselves hurried to the right of the
Union line to fell trees and make slashings that would
shorten the lives of attacking infantry, and afterward
they stood in line behind these slashings with loaded
rifles just in case.

But, as it turned out, there was no attack on this part
of the line. The army huddled in its new camp and
sorted itself out, while McClellan tried to persuade
Abraham Lincoln that what had gone wrong was the
government's fault and not his, and that the army
would never remain loyal or win the war unless the administration dropped all thought of ending slavery and
tried simply to restore the situation as it existed before

the Presidential election of 1860. His success in this
campaign was about equivalent to his success in the
campaign to wrest Richmond away from the protective
hand of General Lee, which is to say that it was a flat
failure. At last the General was ordered to bring his
army back to the vicinity of Washington and get ready
to start all over again.

For a few days, the engineers got something almost
like a rest. To be sure, they had to cross the James at
Coggins' Point to build defensive works in case the
Rebels meant to come in there, mount guns, and shell
the army out of its Harrison's Landing lines, and they
also had to work on the Harrison's Landing works and
keep them too strong for capture. But for a little while,
they had no bridges to build, no roads to make, and no
swamps in which they had to work thigh-deep in water
to construct corduroy roads that would be dislodged by
the next rise in the river levels. There was one organiza-
tional change that seemed to mean a good deal; the
engineer battalion had been composed of three companies, A, B, and C, and now the authorities made up
their minds to have a fourth, Company D, to be made
up of picked men from the other companies and certain
selected soldiers from the volunteer regiments. John
Geyser and his brother, Jacob, were chosen for Company D.

Then, at last, after repeated urging from Washington,
McClellan started his army back down the peninsula to
board the transports at and around Fort Monroe and go
up the Potomac to Washington. The engineers went to
the mouth of the Chickahominy and built the grand-
father of all pontoon bridges to that date, an affair consisting of five spans of trestles and ninety-six pontoon
boats. It was finished on August 14, and the engineers
stood guard with U.S.S. *Pawnee* in the river to guard
against accidents while the Army of the Potomac went
across. On the afternoon of August 18 the army was
over. Within four hours, the engineers had dismantled
the bridge and shipped it on streamers down to Hampton Roads. In due time, the engineers themselves took

ship and went back to Washington, and on September 3 the battalion was in camp again on its original training ground, the open field near the Washington Arsenal. There, while they waited for a new assignment, they noted that there was formal dress parade every evening.

The Mud March

The engineers had about a week of it at the home base—just long enough to get their persons and their uniforms perfectly clean and to live once more in an army where such things were considered important. Then front-line routine returned. General Robert E. Lee took his Confederate army over the Potomac and swung north toward Pennsylvania, his long ragged columns spelling mortal peril for the Republic as they headed for the fat country beyond the mountains. McClellan's army at once took off in pursuit. Like the Confederates, the Unionists were somewhat the worse for wear; unlike the Confederates, they were led by a general who was mistrusted by his government and mistrusted his government in return, and who behaved with unending caution in a situation that offered prizes to the daring.

The Peninsula campaign had left the engineers in poor condition for cross-country marching. The battalion's historian confessed that "we were fairly broken down at one time" and said that for a while it seemed likely that they could not keep up. But after two days they made a good camp near Rockville, Maryland, where fresh fruit and vegetables could be had, and there was a two-day breather while each man's baggage was cut to a minimum. Things went better after that, and for a few days the engineers had no bridges to build and no roads to repair—nothing to do but march, and not at the head of the column either. Up ahead the infantry fought and won hard engagements with the Southerners who held the South Mountain passes, Crampton's Gap and Turner's Gap. The engineers were involved in none of it, except that they made a midnight bivouac at Turner's Gap and discovered the next morning that they had slept in the midst of unburied Confederates killed in a battle the day before. They moved out promptly, got mixed up in a traffic jam at Boonsboro, somehow got out of it, and after making a camp for their hospital, trains, and ambulances at Keedysville, they marched on to join the rest of the army on the banks of an inconsequential stream known as Antietam Creek. Here they put two fords in shape for military use, lugging stone to pave the stream bed in soggy places and grading proper runways on either bank. Finally, late at night, they made camp in the woods.

The Battle of Antietam began at earliest daybreak next day—September 17, 1862—and while this was one of the most terrible and deadly battles of the war, the engineers were not really involved. They took up firearms and stood by for most of the day, in case of a Confederate breakthrough, but in the end they were not called on to shoot at anybody and nobody shot at them. At one point, the high command got worried, and all the extra-duty men back at the engineers' parking lot, including the sick men as well as their attendants and the camp guards, were put under arms and rushed to the front. They were not needed, however, and presently they went back to camp. Thus the engineers set an unusual record; they spent the entire day on the field during one of the deadliest fights of the war, getting an intimate view of most of it, and escaped unhurt.

Back to routine again. A few days after the battle, Lee's army retreated to Virginia and the engineers moved to Harpers Ferry, bridging the Potomac again. Then they bridged the Shenandoah as well, and after that they enjoyed a week with nothing to do but guard the bridges. Apparently, this touch of soft living was too much; the battalion's history contains this prim entry for October 8: "The whole battalion was placed in arrest because of too much merry-making the night before."

Purged of sin in due course, they got on with the war.

They moved to Warrenton, Virginia, early in November, glad to be marching after uneventful weeks tending bridges, and a great change in the army's management took place. General McClellan was removed from command and his place was taken by General Ambrose E. Burnside, who possessed one of the most magnificent beards in the history of the United States Army, but whose other claims on fame were less noteworthy. McClellan had won one of the most important battles of the war; his victory at Antietam killed the chance that England and France might presently intervene on the Confederate side, and it also enabled President Lincoln to issue the Emancipation Proclamation, which changed the nature of the entire war and doomed American slavery forever. But McClellan did not really approve of the Proclamation and he did not approve of President Lincoln's ideas about the conduct of the war, and having won his victory, he did not know what to do with it. So the President dismissed him, and from now on it would be a new war.

This touched the battalion of engineers only peripherally. They were professionals and they would dutifully do the bidding of the army commander, no matter what his ideas on slavery and the President might be, and if the commander now was General Burnside, they would go where he told them to go. After a very short time he told them to go east, toward Fredericksburg, with all the rest of the army going along with them, on the theory that Fredericksburg offered a good line of advance toward Richmond. On the night of November 20 the army made camp in and around the town of Falmouth, across the Rappahannock from Fredericksburg and a mile or so upstream. The weather turned wintry, with cold searching winds, and in the engineers' camp not far from army headquarters, the corporals of the guard made the rounds of the sentry posts all night long to make sure that none of the sentries had succumbed to the cold. A day or so like this and then the familiar orders came down: Stand by with the pontoons, because we need to put bridges over that river.

There were to be two sets of bridges: One bridge built a mile and a half below Fredericksburg, and two bridges built farther apart directly opposite the town. By the luck of the draw the engineer battalion was chosen to build the downstream bridge, while the two regiments of volunteer engineers were to build the ones upstream.

The volunteers had much the worse assignment. Directly across the river were warehouses, stores, and other buildings that backed down to the waterfront, and the Confederates had filled these with sharpshooters who got the working parties in the sights of their rifles and opened a deadly fire. The engineers ran back, leaving dead men on the incomplete scaffolding, and the great array of Federal artillery lined up on the high ground overlooking the river pounded Fredericksburg with a merciless bombardment. This ruined a good many buildings but it did not drive out the sharpshooters, who found shelter in the broken foundation walls and heaps of rubble and reopened fire as soon as the engineers tried to resume their work. In the end, the Federals had to use pontoon boats as landing craft, ferrying infantry across the river with much hallooing and a great splashing of oars, and letting the infantry evict the sharpshooters at the point of the bayonet. Finally, the engineers were able to finish the bridges, but it had cost them heavily in casualties.

Downstream things went better, chiefly because there were no buildings along the Confederate side to hide

sharpshooters. There were sharpshooters, to be sure,
but the infantry and artillery fire from the Federals' side
drove them away. A pontoon-landing craft took across
the men who would make the abutments on the Confederate side, and before too long the bridges were
finished. The jobs were always difficult, and although
the engineers here were wet and exhausted when they
withdrew at evening, they had paid no price like the parties upstream had paid. What they remembered most
about this venture, apparently, was their return to camp
at dusk. On the way they passed the waiting columns of
infantry, massed in the gathering night, utterly silent
with eyes staring out of expressionless faces. They were
preparing to cross the river and engage in what they
knew would be a tremendous battle. The immediate
future was laying its fingertips on these lads, and its
touch was icy.

Icy indeed. The big battle was fought the next day,
December 13, and when the awful day ended the Army
of the Potomac had lost 12,000 men. In general, the
part of the army that crossed by the regulars' bridge
downstream got off better than those who crossed upstream. The front-line general downstream was inert
and kept most of his men out of action, and so held the
butcher's bill within bounds; the authorities whose
troops tried to assault the bluffs back of town shoved in
everybody they could lay their hands on. Neither upstream nor downstream did the Federals win anything,
or come close to winning anything, and the losses at
Fredericksburg had to go in the books as lives wasted.

Here again, as at Antietam, John Geyser and his
fellows were at the battle, but not exactly in it. Except
for a small bridgehead guard they stayed on the
Federals' side of the Rappahannock—technically, the
northern bank, although the river has more or less a
north-south configuration at Fredericksburg so that for
a few miles the northern bank was actually east of the
river. Anyway, call it north or call it east, the engineers
stayed there until eight o'clock at night when the firing
had died down, at which time Company D was sent over

to build a couple of trestle bridges over Deep Run, a creek that came into the Rappahannock from the west. The bridges were for the use of the ambulances that were to bring back as many wounded men as could be collected, and very busy they were for the rest of the night. At the engineers' bivouac near the abutments to the Rappahannock pontoon bridge, the men kept fires going so that the wounded men in the ambulances could have hot coffee before going to the northern side and its waiting hospitals. Before dawn on December 16, the army formally confessed failure by returning to its original camps, and the engineers quietly destroyed the pontoon bridges, thus making certain that Lee who had whipped the Federals so decisively would at least be unable to chase them.

Winter quarters were obviously called for, and the engineers buckled down to it. First thing was to build a 600-foot shed for the draft animals, with evergreen boughs along the walls and roof to make it weatherproof. This done, the men could put up quarters for themselves.

They were built regular army style, with the engineers using their skills to provide, for once, for their own comfort. Details went to the woods and groves to cut logs and haul them back to camp, where company streets had been methodically laid out. The huts were built after the manner of log cabins, notched logs fitted together to enclose a room ten feet long by seven feet wide, with side walls five feet high over a floor made of saplings, of split logs, or of boards when any could be found. A ridge pole ran from end to end, seven feet off the floor, and four shelter tent halves were stretched over this, wall to wall; there was a door at one end, and a fireplace at the other, two bunks on each side, and tight gable ends built of odds and ends of hardtack boxes. Each hut provided snug living quarters for four men, with such items of furniture as individual tastes required. Each first sergeant had a hut to himself, first sergeants being grand and noteworthy folk in the regular army; and there were officers' quarters, a guard-house, a hospital, and buildings for quartermasters and commissary stores. Altogether, very neat.

Winter quarters being completed, it seemed there was not much to do but settle down and wait for spring. The pontoons were all sent off to Belle Plain, on the Potomac, and the engineers adjusted themselves to face a quiet winter of off-and-on drilling and the spare-time fabrication of gabions. In the old days, industrious housewives who got together in midafternoon for a round of gossip and some coffee drinking always took their knitting with them, so that even as they enjoyed unwonted idleness, they could keep their hands employed and not come under the reproach of being sinfully idle. The engineers seem to have used gabions in the same way. No one could say that they idled away their time when they were busy making gabions.

But soon there came the discovery that this winter was not going to be like other winters. On December 31, the last day of an ill-omened year, word went about the camp: Pontoon trains were coming up from Belle Plain, and the engineers had better get ready to wrestle with them. Both the army and the administration had lost face because of the Fredericksburg disaster; what had been lost must be regained (even though it was hard to see how all those lost lives could be brought back), and because the end of the year had brought mild weather, the army ought to take a swing at General Lee. Inasmuch as Lee was on the far side of the Rappahannock, this swing would have to go on pontoons, so the great creaking wagons, with their all but unmanageable loads, started down the roads toward the Rappahannock. Naturally, the engineers were out in front to guide and direct the infantry and artillery that were plodding along behind on totally unpaved dirt roads which, as everyone knew, would turn into deep, clinging, paralyzing mud the moment the rain or mushy January snow began. It was also known that this could happen at any moment, and the march had not gone on for three hours before it was seen that the mild weather was deceptive, cruelly treacherous, and a wetness that would go on getting wetter and wetter for a fortnight began to develop.

What followed was an experience that the Army of the Potomac entered in its books as "The Mud March."

It began, in other words, to rain.

First there was a chilly drizzle; then, under darkening skies, a real downpour, whipped into the men's faces by a driving wind that was likely to box the compass every five minutes; and the wagon wheels of the pontoon train sank deeper and deeper into the mud, until by evening they were axle-deep, wagon beds dragging along over primeval silt, and the mule teams getting mired so that they could pull nothing at all. Some teams escaped suffocation in the quicksand only because mud-encased engineers waddled in beside them and held their heads up, but there are records of mule teams going totally out of sight, lost forever in the unforgiving "sacred soil" of the Confederacy's most distinguished state. Some of the infantry in the struggling column, figuring that they were going nowhere in any case and that the whole project would be given up if it finally became clear that the pontoon trains could not be moved, slipped forward in the drenched twilight and pulled linch pins out of the wagon wheel axles. Engineers with fixed bayonets on their rifles were then sent in to stand guard, under orders to bayonet any man found meddling with the wheels. That took care of that, but the wagon trains still made no progress to speak of.

It went on all evening, and all night. Nobody got anywhere, and at dawn the road was so bad and the animals so completely exhausted that even the high command could see that this was hopeless. But it still seemed necessary to get the pontoons down to the river, and what worn-out mules could not do, worn-out engineers perhaps could do. So the men hoisted the pontoons off the wagons and undertook to haul them along over the mud, letting the mules revive if they could. This did not succeed either, and at last the engineers were allowed to make a bivouac of sorts in a pine thicket, where they could make sketchy shelters out of evergreen boughs and start little fires to warm themselves. They managed to get partly dry, and from a nearby artillerists' camp they were able to borrow some hardtack (they had nothing at all to eat of their own) and they settled down to endure a forty-eight-hour rainfall, huddling in soaked overcoats around smoky fires and doubtless making such remarks as seemed pertinent to them.

One way or another, the army got back to Falmouth, the engineers stumbling into their own camp on January 23, utterly worn out. Two of the men died in the hospital from exhaustion and exposure, and the army as a whole suffered heavily. Officers said later that the mud march cost the army as much of a loss in men who died or were made permanently unfit for duty as an ordinary battle would have done. The engineers had little time to meditate on this because after a couple of days' rest they had to go back and pick up all of the pontoons that had been abandoned and bring them to a hill-top parking lot near Falmouth. Also, there were new lines of entrenchments to lay out.

It was at this point that John Geyser's number came up.

Somewhere around the end of January, he was one of a party chosen to ride out with Captain Cross to run lines of survey for a new set of defensive works. Winter had set in, with saturated gray skies and biting winds, a film of ice on the streams. Going forward to plant stakes along the bank of Aquia Creek, Geyser slipped and fell into the water. He was hauled out just before he drowned and was sent back to camp to get dry and warm. The catch was that camp was ten miles away and Geyser was soaking wet and his only way to get to camp was to ride there on his horse. Somehow, he made the trip without losing his life, but his career as an active soldier in the Corps of Engineers was over.

At Falmouth they got him into the hospital, where he got dry clothing, a warm bed, and such medical care as the doctors of that day could provide a candidate for double pneumonia. A bit later he was sent to the

General Hospital at Washington, and from there he was shipped to the hospital at Fort Schuyler, New York, where he seems to have spent most of the spring and summer. In the autumn he was returned to Washington, suffering from an aggravated case of rheumatism crossed with a touch of malaria, and the engineers concluded that they could use him no more. So in the fall of 1863, John Geyser was discharged from the engineers and was enrolled as a member of the Veterans' Reserve Corps.

This corps was invented for men like Geyser; men made too infirm by wounds or illness for active service, but men who wanted to go on serving their country as long as there was a war going on. The organization had been devised sometime in 1862 and it had gotten off to a bad start. It was originally known as the Invalid Corps, and its members were garbed in what some War Department official considered natty uniforms of robin's-egg blue. Neither the name nor the uniform had been well chosen. The rest of the army considered the corps a refuge for certified gold bricks (as in many cases it actually was), the light blue uniforms pleased no one, and the Invalid Corps was so widely derided that a popular campfire song grew up about it. Eventually the name was changed to Veterans' Reserve Corps, a regular blue uniform was adopted, and the deadbeats were ruthlessly combed out. It might be noted, by the way, that a man who was transferred to the Corps from the regular army was almost certain to be a genuinely afflicted soldier and not a malingerer; the regulars had had many years of experience with men who magnified trifling ailments into crippling disabilities, and when they sent a man to the Veterans' Reserve Corps, it can be assumed he was not shamming. This has a particular bearing on Geyser's case. Rheumatism was the favorite malady blamed by the deadbeats for their inability to do duty, simple because it was very hard for a doctor to tell whether or not a patient was faking. In many regiments there were ironclad rules—nobody was given a medical discharge for rheumatism under any circumstances

whatever. If the regulars released John Geyser from
service because rheumatism had laid him out, you may
be sure that the case was as stated. So, in December
1863, Geyser was formally transferred from the
engineers to Company I, 9th Regiment, Veterans'
Reserve Corps.

If it matters, he was classed as a second battalion
man. The V.R.C. was divided into two battalions. In
the first battalion were the men who were almost good
enough to serve in the line—they could stand erect, walk
about, carry and aim a rifle and do other useful things;
they could do guard duty behind the lines, guard
prisoners and prison camps, or serve as clerks or or-
derlies at various army offices in Washington. In battalion two were the men who were in much worse shape.
Clerical duty behind the lines, where a man could spend
all day sitting at a desk wielding no instrument more
deadly than a pen, was about it as far as they were concerned.

Geyser was in the second battalion. His days in the
regular army were over.

Old Soldier

So this was what it came down to at last. There had been that improbable spring in 1861, with a tall light in the sky at dawn and a breeze blowing in from the unseen land of infinite possibilities, deceitfully telling young men that high adventure was about to begin. There had been the crippling anticlimax of a militia regiment called up too soon and wasted by the posturing incompetence of men old enough to know better. And then there had been the regulars, the engineers, who knew exactly what they were about and made the recruit know it too, using him up and wearing him out and finally putting him on the shelf because he had nothing left to give. Now Geyser was a clerk in the office of the Chief of Ordnance at the War Department, filling in his time there while his comrades in the engineer battalion floundered in mud, cut down trees, made roads and built bridges, and erected fortifications all the way from the Rapidan to the James River. For them, as for him, the glamour had departed. More accurately, it had never really existed. It was composed of things as insubstantial as the frost patterns on a northern window pane, it was felt and imagined but never actually seen or experienced, and when it had gone forever, a man could call himself a veteran.

By this time, the men knew what was happening to them. In June of 1864, Jacob Geyser, John's younger brother, was with the engineers when they made a bivouac at Dispatch Station on the way down to the James. The men remarked that they had been there before, two years ago, when the peninsular campaign was yet to be worked out, and the dullest man could see that there had been a great change. The battalion's historian cried passionately: "How many good men had been literally worn out in the two years! Not an officer of that day [May 22, 1862] was still on duty with the battalion!" You can always tell an official historian in the army by the fact that he tells his story in terms of officers. A great many enlisted men had been worked out, thrown away, and replaced in those two years, but the man who wrote the history was thinking of the shoulder straps. The likes of John Geyser are not mentioned.

Well, maybe he did not miss it. He was an old soldier now, starting down the long sunset slope that is reserved for old soldiers, moving into the years of peace under a strange and crippling handicap. With half a century to live, the great climax of his life was already behind him.

Perhaps it is not that way anymore. The Civil War had some unplesant after effects, but at least it did not infect its veterans with the virus of self-pity. It was not followed by a generation of serious thinkers who kept assuring the ex-soldier that he had wasted his time. The army itself, badly organized and erratically led as it so often was, had at least given him something he did not get in time of peace—a memory of binding comradeship, of cruel duties that looked less cruel in retrospect because they had been shared with his fellows, the sharing creating a tie that no man could break or would wish to break. Anyone who has followed the story of Civil War veterans after Appomattox is bound to be struck by a singular thing: Disliking war itself and having no taste for a return of its dangers and infamous pains, the veterans nevertheless wanted—more seemingly than they wanted anything else—to re-create their old life together, to reenter the strange world they once knew in which at peril of their own lives they were joined intimately to each other's. The piping times of peace had taught them that this does not happen very often; but it had happened to them once, and they never could keep from looking back to it.

No matter. John Geyser's health seems to have improved, and in the spring of 1864 he was reclassified as a first battalion man, meaning that he was judged fit to move about and be moderately active. He was sent to David's Island in New York harbor to serve as a clerk at DeCamp General Hospital. Later on, he was transferred back to Washington for duty in some headquarters' office. At last, on September 13, 1864, his term of service having expired, he was discharged, paid in full, and sent back to Allegheny City to start life over again.

At this point we almost lose sight of him. Even as a soldier he was anonymous, never coming out of the skyline to come into proper focus, except for the personality that can be glimpsed in those sketches that he put in his little book. Starting life all over again after four years of war is a good trick if you can do it, but the record one leaves is thin and insubstantial. Most of us leave few traces. Away from the army, John Geyser left hardly any. It has been written that the country whose annals are poor is happy. Perhaps the same is true of human beings. Geyser may have been happy.

Here and there he touched recognizable milestones.

Not long after he got back to Allegheny City—on January 1, 1865—he married Miss Abbie M. Tillett. It is permissible to suppose that this represented a prewar attachment, with some understanding reached by wartime letters. In any case, they seem to have made a good marriage of it. It lasted until her death on August 13, 1899, and she bore him two sons who survived her: John, born in 1866, and George, born in 1870.

On his release from the army, Geyser had gone back
to his trade, and eventually he opened a little shop in
Allegheny City, supporting himself and his family well
enough through several postwar decades. But in the '90s
the rheumatism that had ended his career with the
engineers overtook him again, with painful results that
are recited in his file of papers at the Pension Bureau.
Within six months of his wife's death, Geyser filed a
claim for a pension for service-connected disability.

Geyser's family doctor died and he had no physician—not that any physician then could do very much
for a rheumatic—so Geyser turned to drugs, meaning
patent medicines, for relief. He got no relief, and at last
he said that he "made up my mind to endure what I
could not cure," gave up the medications, and did his
best to make his own way. But his condition obviously
was not good; he became very fat and his muscles
deteriorated. He was often disabled for days at a time
and at last had to close his shop. An associate filed an
affidavit saying that Geyser "is able only to do such
light work as his friends can give him, his own time and
convenience to carry out." He was, in short, a played-
out old soldier, and he needed help. The Pension
Bureau saw it that way, and he was classified as "invalid" and given a pension of $15 a month.

The records of the Pension Bureau are terse, and all
that we know of this man's career after the war comes
from the Bureau's files. The last entry of all is dated
September 28, 1908. Under the heading "Pensioner
dropped," it certifies that John Geyser, one-time Artificer in Company D, U. S. Engineers, has been removed from the rolls "because of death."

So, there is the soldier's story. Its moments of drama
are few. Somewhere along the line, the ardent youngster
who hurried to the recruiting officer the moment the
guns at Fort Sumter had cooled became the old man
who shut up his shop and had to ask for a pension, and
we do not really know very much of the story. We iden-
tify him with the great cause he served and we know him
as part of a greater whole. Then he becomes a civilian

again, and we lose him. Proving that the soldier is more interesting than the civilian?

Not necessarily. As a member of one of earth's unnumbered generations he represents something grander than any army: humanity itself, working without glamour and without reward to make its painful, never-ending progress from one everlasting mystery to another, hoping and suffering and enduring, its capacity for all of these being infinite. In this pageant, too vast to be seen or understood, he had the same sort of part as you and I.

PART SIX

Visions

_____

A Dark Indefinite Shore

I began my work on the Civil War by trying to figure out what made the old veterans tick when they were young men. It was as simple as that. I was trying to turn the old men I had known into vigorous, young soldiers. That carried me quite a distance, but it could not have taken me through years of endeavor because, after all, that feeling you could satisfy quite easily.

The trouble is, as I got deeper and deeper into the war, there were more things I wanted to know. I wanted to know what motivated the people on both sides; why both North and South carried such terribly heavy burdens throughout the war, with really a minimum of complaining. When you read about a battle like Spotsylvania Court House, for instance, with its perfectly appalling tales of suffering, bloodshed, and death on both sides, all concentrated into one rainy summer morning along the edge of a second-growth forest, you are bound to be stirred by certain questions: What motivated the men on both sides? What drove them into

that? What kept them at it? What prevented them from
running away? I'm not sure that I know the answers yet,
but have come to the conclusion that the American man
is a pretty good man, no matter what part of the country
he comes from. When he sets himself to do something,
he will stick with it as long as he can stand on his feet
and breathe.

But you must go beyond even that. You conduct your
own examination into the war and you arrive, finally, at
the questions: What did it do for us, what did it accomplish? Was it simply a waste, a needless, violent
episode that broke our country apart? Was it something
that should have been avoided or did we get something
out of it? I suppose it took me a long time to fumble my
way through questions like those, but I did finally come
to the conclusion, and I grow stronger in it every day,
that the war was worthwhile, that it did accomplish
something. It gave us a political unity in the sense that it
kept the country from fragmenting into a number of
separate, independent nations. The North American
continent was not Balkanized; the geographic unit that
made possible the wealth and the prosperity of later
days was preserved. Beyond that, the country made
a commitment during that war; a commitment to a
broader freedom, a broader citizenship. We can no
longer be content with anything less than complete
liberty, complete equality before law for all of our people regardless of their color, their race, their religion,
their national origins; regardless of anything. We all
have to fare alike. We are fated to continue the experiment in peaceful democracy, and I don't think any people were ever committed to a nobler experiment than
that one.

So I can't help feeling that the war was worth its cost.
We have not yet reached the goal we set ourselves at the
time, and I'm not sure we ever will be satisfied with our
progress. But at least we keep going. We have to continue on the path that was laid out for us at Appomattox, and it is a very good path for any people to
follow.

That surrender at Appomattox was one of the most important moments in American history. A great deal of emotion attaches itself to the scene we see there, particularly in the South. When Lee left Appomattox Court House to ride through his surrendered army and the men tried to cheer him and broke into tears instead, he rode straight into legend. He took the army with him, and to this day, Lee and the Army of Northern Virginia live in legend to an extent that none of the Northern soldiers or armies succeeded in doing.

It seems to me that that fact is one of the best things that ever happened to the United States, for this reason: The men of the Southern Confederacy had fought a four-year civil war; they had fought it to the limit of their ability; they had lost. Some of the things Northern armies did on Southern soil were not calculated to make the Southern people love them. All in all, the people of the South had been through a hard, bitter experience.

A civil war is, of all wars, the kind most likely to leave angry feelings; irreconcilably angry feelings. In Ireland, in France, in practically any place you name, an extended civil war has left a very uneasy peace. Often enough, it has left a peace that is not really a peace at all, with shootings at crossroads by night, with violence breaking out here and there, with the populace not in the least reconciled to defeat, and grimly anxious to carry on the struggle against the hated foe, in any way possible.

That did not happen in this country. There was bitterness in the South, to be sure. There was a feeling that still sends echoes across the body politic from time to time, but there was nothing like the incurable hatred and enmity that are ordinarily left behind by civil wars.

The Southerners were not going to resign themselves to defeat. They wanted to go ahead in any way possible, and yet, in the end there was peace.

I think the chief reason for this is the legend of Robert E. Lee and the heroic Confederate soldiers. For this legend was the channel through which pent-up emotions could be discharged. The essence of the legend of Lee and the dauntless Confederate soldiers was that they suffered mightily in a great but lost cause. The point is that this very phrase accepts the cause as having been lost. There was no hint in this legend of biding one's time and waiting for a moment when there could be revenge. This was the lost cause; something to be cherished, to be revered, to be the outlet for emotions, but not to be the center of a new outbreak of violence.

In that sense, I think the legend of the lost cause has served the entire country very well. The things that were done during the Civil War have not been forgotten, of course, but we now see them through a veil. We have elevated the entire conflict to a realm where it is no longer explosive. It is a part of American legend, a part of American history, a part, if you will, of American romance. It moves men mightily, to this day, but it does not move them in the direction of picking up their guns and going at it again. We have had national peace since the war ended, and we will always have it, and I think the way Lee and his soldiers conducted themselves in the hours of surrender has a great deal to do with it.

As it happened, Abraham Lincoln did not live to see the war end. He did know about Lee's surrender, and he knew, of course, that the war would very soon be over. He did not, however, see it end.

On the morning of April 14, Lincoln had a cabinet meeting in the White House. Everybody was feeling relaxed because Lee had surrendered, and Lincoln remarked that they were going to get big news somehow in the next twenty-four hours. His Cabinet members wanted to know what made him think so. He said he had had a dream. It was a recurrent dream that he had frequently during the war, and every time he had it, it foreshadowed some great event—a huge battle, a big victory, a political move of some kind. Well, of course, people wanted to know what the dream was like, and Lincoln said it was rather mysterious. In this dream, he was on some sort of boat, moving rapidly forward over a dim, hazy sea toward, as he put it, a dark and indefinite shore. In the dream, he had never actually reached the shore, but when he woke up, he knew that big news, a big development of some kind, was about to take place.

He was quite right. That night, he went to Ford's Theatre, and less than twenty-four hours after he told about his dreams, he was dead. He had, presumably, reached that dark, indefinite shore. He left his country with the war won, moving likewise on a mysterious vessel across a mysterious sea, toward a dark, indefinite shore. There was no chart for that shore, because nobody had ever been there. We still don't have a chart, but we are still on our way. We are crossing the seas on which the Civil War put us afloat. Like Lincoln, we are moving toward a destiny bigger than we can understand. The dark, indefinite shore is still ahead of us. Maybe we will get there some day if we live up to what the great men of our past won for us. And when we get there, it is fair to suppose that instead of being dark and indefinite, that unknown continent will be lit with sunlight.

Notes on
the Illustrations

FRONTISPIECE
(Untitled)

When the young recruits on both sides first got to camp, they were all in a great hurry to get to the front. A lot of them were scared the war was going to end before they got into action. But by the winter of 1862—after the terrible battles of Antietam, Gaines' Mills, Seven-days Battle, and Fredericksburg—John Geyser and the men around him had changed. The boys were a little withdrawn. They weren't quite so bubbly. The first battle had shaken them down very much. After that, you never heard them talk about being impatient to get into action. Any troops who talked that way were fresh from the training camp. It took a few months to wash away the stardust. Like this young soldier, they began to get that far-away lost look in their eyes—thinking of so many places they'd rather be than in the army.

ONE

The cover of John B. Geyser's sketchbook. On it he drew his bedroll and gear, and identified his outfit: Company D, U. S. Engineers. On the inside of the cover he inscribed his home address (*33 Arm Str., Allegheny City, Allegheny Co., Pa),* and the date he received the book, *Jan. 25th, 1862.* The label of the store from which the book was purchased is still intact and tells us that it came from *Art & Artists' Emporium, Goupil & Co., 772 Broadway, New York.*

TWO
Working in Chickahominy River outside of the Pickets

This sketch, made just before the Seven-days Battle, shows a detail of soldiers making a bridge over the Chickahominy River outside of Richmond. They are mostly regular line infantrymen with engineers directing the work. The soldiers are up to their knees, or deeper, cutting down trees and rafting logs together; one man has just fallen in.

The Union Army was on the north side of the river and had to cross it to get to Richmond, which was only about six or seven miles away. Ordinarily, the Chickahominy was not much of a stream, and you could easily wade across. But it flowed through very low ground, and a day or two of solid rain thirty or forty miles upstream would turn it into a torrent. When that happened, you had to have a bridge to get across, and the surrounding swamp became a shallow, muddy lake.

THREE
Outpost on Chickahominy   *June 25th, 1862*

This ia a very realistic scene of soldiers relaxing and
playing cards at an outpost along the Chickahominy
River. It's a little hard for us to imagine today, but
playing cards was considered wicked in those days . . .
cards were tools of the devil. When there was a big battle coming up and the boys knew it, the routes to the
place where they were going to fight would be littered
with decks of cards they had thrown away. A man
didn't want to be shot with a deck of cards in his pocket,
just as in more recent years, a soldier might throw away
a sheaf of dirty pictures just in case he was killed and
they sent his effects to the next of kin. He wouldn't
want his wife or mother looking at them.

FOUR
(Untitled)

This is a typical cook camp. Note the cooking fire with a
bucket hanging over it, the table, stool, and the soldier
unpacking hardtack from a box labeled "U.S.A.
Bread." The man sauntering around with the bayoneted
musket on his shoulder is on guard duty.

Nobody was ever enlisted in the army in the Civil War
specifically as a cook. Men were detailed from the
ranks, or simply split the duty and took turns. Some of
the messes that were concocted were pretty awful, which
is one reason for high rate of sickness that afflicted the
army.

FIVE
Out of the Tent   Novbr. 25, 1862

The Civil War soldiers formed groups, or "messes" as they were called, who tented together. One soldier would carry the coffeepot, another would carry the stew bucket or frying pan, and so on. Together, they had what they needed for cooking.

Each soldier, of course, had a tin cup that held a little less than a quart, and he carried that with him at all times in his haversack. In that, he would have coffee. Whenever the army halted, he would fill the cup with water, put it on the fire, shake some coffee into it, and in a couple of minutes he would have boiled coffee.

The forming of "messes" happened naturally. The soldiers weren't under orders to do so, it was just a matter of being around the men you liked. They became fiercely loyal to each other.

SIX AND SEVEN
City of Fredericksburg   Novbr. 29th, 1862
Drawn by J. B. Geyser

This is a full-dress sketch of the Town of Fredericksburg, drawn on November 27. The two armies glowered at each other there for two weeks or more before the Union Army and John Geyser's company of engineers finally laid pontoon bridges and went across, where they got very badly beaten.

On the day these sketches were made, the Union advance had reached Fredericksburg. If they had been able to cross then, they could have taken control of the town and the road leading south from it, which was what they really wanted, at practically no expense, for there were few Confederates in the town. The bridges had been wrecked, however, and in order to build new ones they had to have the pontoon train—but the pontoon train was up in Maryland.

Although the orders to bring the pontoon train down had already been issued, it was slow in arriving. Some of the army sat for about ten days waiting for it, while Lee's army marched into Fredericksburg and took possession of the hills around it. By the time the Yankees were ready to build their bridges, the attempt to seize the town was hopeless. Even before the major battle a great many men were killed in the bridge-building process. The Confederate riflemen took refuge in that old mill and on the lower floors of the other waterfront buildings, and from these concealed quarters they shot at the engineers.

EIGHT
Pickets in the River

Soldiers spent a lot of their time on picket duty, and it was a long and lonely job. It's getting near wintertime here, so the soldiers have their coats on. That pouch on the picket's belt holds cartridges. The Civil War cartridge was a lead bullet with a paper tube attached to one end for the powder. To load the gun, you bit off the end of the paper cone, poured the powder down the barrel and sent the bullet down after it, ramming it down with a ram rod. Then you took a copper cap out of your small box and capped the nipple of the rifle, just the way a child puts a cap in a toy pistol nowadays. The rifle was then ready to be fired.

NINE
(Untitled)

This battle scene shows a squad of infantry chasing a Confederate cavalry outpost away from the house. The officer is waving his cap, as was often done, so that his soldiers could see the place to rally around. The company flag served the same purpose.

If a soldier was killed, as is depicted here, his company officer would send a letter home and would see to it that his belongings were rounded up. The tentmates would usually write also, but it was up to the company officer to see that the next of kin was properly notified.

The dead soldier would most likely be buried on the spot, a wooden marker with his name and regiment on it marking the grave. Then, a year or two later, he would be exhumed and put into a proper military cemetery. Many boys were worried about getting properly identified before burial. When a big fight was coming up, a concerned soldier would take a little piece of paper and write his name and his company and regiment on it and pin it to his coat. If he was shot, the guys who came out to look after their men would at least know who he was.

TEN
Down the cannall (sic) *from Our Tent*

The canal referred to here is the Chesapeake and Potomac Canal, which runs right beside the Potomac River and up past Harpers Ferry. The peacefulness of this scene belies the bloodiness that was just ahead, on the nearby battlefield at Antietam.

ELEVEN
(Untitled)

The Army of the Potomac never did quite solve the problem of stragglers. They were very proud of their marching discipline and thought themselves a cut above the western armies, but they straggled worse, which is usually a sign of ineffective discipline. The men in the drawing are men who fell out and will probably eventually pick up their guns and go on to rejoin their outfits. Not all stragglers did, however; some of them stayed out.

TWELVE
Yorktown   April 30th, 1862

These Union soldiers were called Zouaves. The Zouave uniform was a combination of French and oriental design and looked like nothing anybody had ever seen in America. At the start of the war, the uniform was very popular with a lot of soldiers, for it wasn't every day that a young man from the country got to wear baggy red pants with white gaiters, a blue jacket, and a Turkish fez on top of his head. The colorful uniforms were quickly abandoned, however, when the boys discovered what good targets they made.

THIRTEEN
(Untitled)

The veteran cavalryman learned that the thing to do with a saber was not to hit the other man with it; it was to stick him with it. Unless you hit him in the face, slashing almost certainly wouldn't do any lasting damage. If you plunged the thing into him, you could end his life. In 1864 Confederate Bedford Forrest, who probably was the best cavalryman and one of the hardest fighters of the whole war, got into a fight just like the one pictured here. He and a young Union officer struggled, just as these two are struggling, and Forrest finally got the better of him. A few days later, he was talking to a Union officer who had come into camp under a flag of truce to deliver a message, and they got to talking about that fight. The officer asked him about

it and Forrest said, "You know, if that young feller had
had sense enough to give me the point, I wouldn't be
here right now, but he tried to cut, which was his last
mistake."

FOURTEEN AND FIFTEEN
Our Tent 1892
G. Thompson C. H. Rice Jacob Geyser, Jr.
J. B. Geyser
Decbr. 28th, 1862

This is an extremely interesting set of portraits of the
tentmates who lived with John Geyser, including a self-
portrait. The name of the man next to John Geyser is
also Geyser—Jacob Geyser, Jr.—his brother. They
enlisted together and lived and fought together.

The feeling of comradeship that grew among the
soldiers during the war was quite powerful. Sometimes
it seemed that it was the strongest emotion they had,
even stronger than the patriotism that had led them out
there. It held a lot of those regiments together when they
otherwise would have fallen apart.

If you look carefully at these sketches, there is that
haunted, lost look in the eyes which, I suppose, has appeared on the face of every soldier since the day of
Julius Caesar's Legions. It comes through, perhaps, in
spite of the artist. The drawing is dated December 28,
1862. They've got the Battle of Fredericksburg behind
them, and that was enough to haunt anybody's eyes.

SIXTEEN
J.B.G. Decbr. 4th, 1862

This eloquent picture was drawn on December 4, 1862,
not long before the Battle of Fredericksburg. The young
man is a million miles from there, though; he's back

wherever it was he came from, back home. It is, I think, the saddest of John Geyser's drawings. For a brief moment, the soldier has escaped the army—but he knows it is only a reprieve.

Index

Abolitionists, 5, 6, 9, 15, 85
Alabama, 8, 20. *See also*
  specific battles, places
Albermarle (ship), 137
Anaconda Plan, 20, 25
Anderson, Robert, 76
Andersonville Prison (Georgia)
  67-68
Antietam, Md., Battle of, 29,
  87-88, 207, 208
Antietam Creek, Md., 169, 207
Appomattox Courthouse, Va.,
  Lee's surrender at, 120-21,
  227-28
Armistead, Lewis, 35
Army of the Potomac, 26, 69,
  82-98, 99-108, 109-14, 115-21,
  176, 178, 181, 182, 196, 204,
  206ff., *(see also* specific
  battles, individuals, places);
  volunteer reenlistments in, 61-
  62
Artillery, 128, 129-30, 193-94
Atlanta, Ga., march on and
  capture of, 105, 111, 113-14,
  117, 140, 141, 142

Balloons, hydrogen, use of, 133
Baltimore, Md., 32-33
Baltimore and Ohio Railroad,
  169, 171

Banks, Nathaniel P., 104, 105,
  182, 184, 185
Beauregard, P. G. T., 100, 149-
  50, 169-70, 172
Blacks, 5, 7, 11ff. *(see also*
  Slavery); as Civil War troops,
  16-17, 119; N.Y.C. draft riots
  and, 58
Blockade, 19-23, 25, 77, 84, 99-
  100, 134, 138, 145-46;
  runners, 22, 138, 146; and
  wartime trade, 144-45
Booth, John Wilkes, 29
Bounties, volunteers and, 60-61;
  bounty jumpers and, 60-61
Bragg, Braxton, 101, 104, 109-
  11, 150
Bridges (bridge building),
  engineers and, 176, 177, 182-
  85, 188-90, 198-203, 204, 208,
  209-10, 233-34
British. *See* Great Britain
Brown, John, 10
Buckner, Simon B., 106
Buell, Don Carlos, 101
Bull Run, Battle of, 78-80, 172;
  Henry House Hill, 78, 80;
  second, 84, 86
Burnside, Ambrose E., 89-90,
  111, 208
Butler, Ben, 11-13, 17

239

TRUE ACCOUNTS OF VIETNAM
from those who returned to tell it all . . .

___PHANTOM OVER VIETNAM: FIGHTER PILOT, USMC John Trotti
0-425-10248-3/$3.95

___SURVIVORS: AMERICAN POWS IN VIETNAM Zalin Grant
0-425-09689-0/$3.95

___THE KILLING ZONE: MY LIFE IN THE VIETNAM WAR Frederick Downs
0-425-10436-2/$3.95

___AFTERMATH Frederick Downs
Facing life after the war
0-425-10677-2/$3.95

___NAM Marc Baker
The Vietnam War in the words of the soliders who fought there.
0-425-10144-4/$3.95

___BROTHERS: BLACK SOLDIERS IN THE NAM Stanley Goff and
Robert Sanders with Clark Smith
0-425-10648-9/$3.50

___INSIDE THE GREEN BERETS Col. Charles M. Simpson III
0-425-09146-5/$3.95

___THE GRUNTS Charles R. Anderson
0-425-10403-6/$3.50

___THE TUNNELS OF CU CHI Tom Mangold and John Penycate
0-425-08951-7/$3.95

___AND BRAVE MEN TOO Timothy S. Lowry
The unforgettable stories of Vietnam's Medal of Honor winners.
0-425-09105-8/$3.95

Check book(s). Fill out coupon. Send to:

BERKLEY PUBLISHING GROUP
390 Murray Hill Pkwy., Dept. B
East Rutherford, NJ 07073

NAME_____

ADDRESS_____

CITY_____

STATE_____ZIP_____

PLEASE ALLOW 6 WEEKS FOR DELIVERY.
PRICES ARE SUBJECT TO CHANGE
WITHOUT NOTICE.

POSTAGE AND HANDLING:
$1.00 for one book, 25¢ for each additional. Do not exceed $3.50.

BOOK TOTAL	$_____
POSTAGE & HANDLING	$_____
APPLICABLE SALES TAX (CA, NJ, NY, PA)	$_____
TOTAL AMOUNT DUE	$_____

PAYABLE IN US FUNDS.
(No cash orders accepted.)

247